WHAT THE ICE GETS

ALSO BY MELINDA MUELLER

Apocrypha
Asleep in Another Country
Private Gallery

WHAT THE ICE GETS

Shackleton's Antarctic Expedition, 1914–1916

{ A POEM }

Melinda Mueller

VAN WEST & COMPANY · SEATTLE

Library of Congress Card Number: 00-107900
ISBN 0-9677021-1-9
Second Printing, 2001
9 8 7 6 5 4 3 2

Cover art: Untitled photograph (Antarctic ice field), by Jim and Lisa Mastro.
Copyright © 1999 by Artville, LLC.

Grateful acknowledgment is made to the following for permission to reprint excerpts from previously published or recorded material.

BBC: Excerpt from *Walking Out of History: The True Story of Shackleton's Endurance Expedition.* American Radio Works, 1999. Minnesota Public Radio. Used by permission of the BBC Rights Archive.

CAEDMON OF WHITBY PUBLISHERS: Excerpt from *Frank Wild* by Leif Mills. Copyright © 1999 by Leif Mills. Used by permission of Caedmon of Whitby Publishers.

CURTIS BROWN, LTD.: Excerpts from *Endurance: Shackleton's Incredible Voyage* by Alfred Lansing. Copyright © 1959 by Alfred Lansing. Reprinted by permission of Curtis Brown, Ltd.

FARRAR, STRAUS & GIROUX, LLC: Excerpt from Homer, *The Odyssey,* translated by Robert Fitzgerald. Copyright © 1961, 1963 by Robert Fitzgerald. Copyright renewed 1989 by Benedict R. C. Fitzgerald, on behalf of the Fitzgerald children. Reprinted by permission of Farrar, Straus & Giroux, LLC.

NATIONAL GEOGRAPHIC SOCIETY: Excerpts from *Shackleton: The Antarctic Challenge* by Kim Heacox. Copyright © 1999 by the National Geographic Society. Used by permission of the National Geographic Society.

W. W. NORTON & COMPANY, INC.: Excerpts from *Endurance: An Epic of Polar Adventure* by F. A. Worsley. Copyright © 1931 by the Estate of F. A. Worsley. Used by permission of W. W. Norton & Company, Inc. Excerpts from *Shackleton's Boat Journey* by F. A. Worsley. Copyright © 1977 by W. W. Norton & Company, Inc. Used by permission of W. W. Norton & Company, Inc.

TRAFALGAR SQUARE PUBLISHING AND EBURY PRESS: Excerpts from *South: The Story of Shackleton's Last Expedition 1914-1917* by Ernest Shackleton, edited and annotated by Peter King. Editorial material copyright © 1991 by Peter King. Used by permission of Trafalgar Square Publishing and Ebury Press.

VAN WEST & COMPANY, PUBLISHERS
5341 Ballard Avenue NW
Seattle, Washington 98107
www.vanwestco.com

Contents

Foreword

SEE THIS SINGLE WOODEN SHIP, one of the stoutest ever built by a Norwegian shipwright, entering a young century not yet marred by war, entering a long summer day with no darkness ahead for months. It is entering brash and bergs and pack ice, miles of ice too thick to plow through or smash or cut with axes and saws. Crystal air so cold even in summer that ice, "like tiny stars," hangs in cloudless skies. When the ice finally gets its way, this ship might as well be anchored in a Nebraska cornfield for all the progress it will make without a miracle.

Picture a wrinkled white cloth on a huge banquet table; drop one grain of black pepper on it. If there were aircraft capable of flying over the ice in 1915, the scene below would look like that. There sits the *Endurance*, Shackleton's ship, speared by lances of ice, the ice then doing whatever it is the ice pleases to do with her. But there are no planes capable of such flights, and no radios to reach anywhere beyond right here, no way for anyone to know the jeopardy of twenty-eight men stranded, and only ordeals ahead.

Then see these men, eleven scientists and seventeen seamen, a very human mix of sensitivity to their comrades' slights, courage, and fear. All of them possess a wild ability to endure misery. The leaders among them—Sir Ernest Shackleton, Frank Worsley, and Frank Wild—are built from unflagging will, intelligence, knowledge, resourcefulness, experience, courage, a humor the ice cannot imprison, and, yes, that capacity for endurance. As polar explorer Apsley Cherry-Garrard said, "For scientific discovery, give me Scott; for speed and efficiency of travel, give me Amundsen; but when disaster strikes and all hope is gone, get down on your knees and pray for Shackleton."

At the other end of the century, we find a poet with similar capacities for her own life and work. She has the skills and craftsmanship to master various forms from free verse to heroic couplets, the psychological and spiritual insight to understand the working of men's hearts, and the scientific training to understand our natural world. Leave her to explore this experience in the ice. Together this landscape, these men bound to this place, and this poet constitute the ingredients for epic.

In every culture poetry has been used to tell great stories. Not only the Greeks but the Ainu, the Norse, the Lakota, the Icelandic peoples come immediately to mind. We have told our histories both great and small — from Homer's *Iliad* to Coleridge's "The Rime of the Ancient Mariner" — in verse ranging from classical Greek forms to the meters of ballads and hymns. Now we have Shackleton's saga in a poetry as various in its forms as the Antarctic ice, but more reliable. The history is as accurate as good scholarship can make it, and the beauty and terror of the events are brought to vivid life.

Melinda Mueller's poem begins with birds. These birds are like tales springing up from the page, and "The mind rises with them as they rise…." The poem ends with birds, far off in South Africa, where "A man who was a hero / tends a squalid bar…" and the "Red-billed wood hoopoes up- / end themselves on their perches, tails / flung uppermost, / and give out cackling whoops of laughter," as if both Nature and stories are so filled with painful ironies that even the birds mock us and laugh at our foolishness. Mueller's story shows us the continuities between humans and landscapes, humans and stories, landscapes and stories, and the importance of each.

Her poetic skills enable each man on the expedition to address us in a distinct voice. The narrator speaks in iambic pentameter that drives us inexorably along.

> They steamed out from Grytviken from the sight
> of the world, dissolving into gray sleet….

> …the green sea turns abruptly indigo
> and then there's ice, farther north than usual.

The voices of the scientists and seamen have their own literary styles: four-line stanzas with the second and fourth rhyming; or long, looping twelve-, fifteen-, or even eighteen-syllable lines in rhyming couplets; alternating prose-poem stanzas and rhymed stanzas — whatever the form, each exhibits the utmost craft. Thus Thomas Crean, who had been with Scott:

> One thing, I'd like to stand
> at the Pole. I was that close

I could have shouted at it, and when
Scott turned us back and chose

the other team for the last push,
I'm not ashamed to say
it was a blow brought me to tears.
We watched them march away....

Harry McNeish and Frank Hurley speak in couplets, the end-rhymes so carefully chosen they are subdued, so unobtrusive you can read a whole page before you become aware that the rhyme is there, never a hint that the form is driving the poem, or that a word was chosen because it rhymes. And the poetry is never without drama; the narrative and the individual stories within it carry us along. McNeish says:

Well 'tis all up with the ship the Ice has cut clean
Through her & next thing the Boss sends Mr Crean

To do away with the cat as the Boss says we can keep
But two pounds each besides our clothes. He makes a heap

Of his own things & shows us gold coins in his palm
Then throws them down & tears the 23rd Psalm

Out of his Bible & lays the Bible on the Ice to make
His point.

Wild, who keeps everyone's spirits up with his steady demeanor and tireless optimism, speaks in stanzas of three long lines, the first and last lines rhyming:

I tell the others it would be absurd to think that Providence
would give up on us now, having already put Itself to such
a deal of trouble for our sakes. Just look at the evidence

of all our close escapes. What was the good of those,
I tell them, if we're not meant to live? That God hears our prayers
has been already proved—if not always in the manner we suppose.

It is part of Mueller's achievement that the form of each voice becomes the person; we recognize the voice and immediately know and care about each man, come to recognize his foibles and his strengths.

The voices of other great characters, like the ice in its crunches and bellows and sighs, reach us clearly. And the wind's capacity to move all that ice, to drive boats through contrary currents, to roll a fallen man before it so that he cannot regain his feet: the wind acquires here a most eloquent voice.

And then there is the story itself. Twenty-eight men bound for Antarctica to cross the continent, "and claim that feat / for Britain and themselves." But they run into unseasonal ice far north of their destination. On January 19, 1915, the *Endurance* is lodged in the ice and the men are at the mercy of the floes. Ship and men drift ten months, and then the ice simply stoves everything in, the ship goes under, and the men are left stranded on the shifting floes. Living on penguin and seal, they find ways to fill the endless day with tasks to avoid panic, boredom, insanity, thoughts of home or of suicide. When the ice finally breaks, they launch the three lifeboats salvaged from the *Endurance*. They will row and sail and finally fetch up on Elephant Island, a place of windy gales, narrow rocky beach, high sea cliffs and mountains, and nothing whatever of civilization. "There was no hope of rescue by others," wrote Worsley, the captain of the *Endurance*, later. They opted to risk the lives of a few to save the lives of the rest.

Shackleton would sail in the twenty-two-and-a-half-foot-long *James Caird* with five carefully selected crewmen to South Georgia Island, a speck amid the worst winds, currents, and seas the world has to offer. Using celestial navigation between storms, Worsley guided them the eight hundred miles to get there. High seas forced them to crash-land on an uninhabited part of the island. From there they climbed mountains and slid down glaciers, avoiding crevasses, until they finally walked like filthy ghosts into the whaling station. Shackleton eventually found a ship that could sail back through the ice and every man was saved — at least for a time.

The world had changed in their absence. The first Great War was raging and two men of this expedition promptly died in it. Nothing would ever again be the same for the world or for these men. They lived to perish elsewhere, and Mueller raises the appropriate and challenging questions about what that irony might mean. Regardless, the story reveals again the most compelling essentials of our own endurance for the tests that life brings, and in our time of diminished heroes reminds us that genuine heroism is possible.

GARY HOLTHAUS
June 2000

Preface

I HAVE THIS MEMORY from childhood: I am visiting the home of schoolmates in Spokane, Washington — three girls all within two years of my age. Their grandmother stands in the hall, a white-haired woman in a smart blue dress. Grandma Shackleton. My friends did not know how they might be related to Ernest Shackleton, but they told me about him with the pride children have in famous relatives. Thanks to them I devoured Alfred Lansing's wonderful retelling of the most remarkable of Shackleton's voyages, the voyage of the *Endurance*.

Since then I have rediscovered this story many times — great stories have that capacity, to wait for us to catch up to them again. I have sat beside a campfire above the Arctic Circle, in such drenching twenty-four-hour light as Shackleton and his men knew at the other Pole, and listened while Frank Worsley's account of the voyage was read aloud. After a diagnosis of cancer, I found myself reading and rereading Caroline Alexander's book about the *Endurance* expedition, with its reproductions of Frank Hurley's extraordinary photographs. I often thought that if the men of the *Endurance* could do what they had done, I could very well get through what I was facing. I would turn to Hurley's photographic portrait of Frank Wild, in which Wild looks what they all said he was — imperturbable down to his bones — and I borrowed some of that calm.

My treat to myself after completing chemotherapy was to fly to New York and see an exhibit on Shackleton's expedition, mounted by the American Museum of Natural History. Standing beside the *James Caird*, which had carried Shackleton and his men to rescue (and which I felt had carried me, too, for the previous several months), I had the thought that it was odd no one had ever written the story as a poem. It is, after all, an epic tale of heroic and motley characters in a fabulous landscape. I thought, also, that writing such a poem would give me another opportunity to keep company with this story. It proved to be a fine companion for all the months spent writing it.

Shackleton's plan for the *Endurance* expedition was to land with a shore party on the Weddell Sea side of Antarctica, and then to cross the continent, passing over the South Pole (a feat that would not actually be accomplished until decades later). This plan required that a second party land on the Ross Sea coastline and lay depots of fuel and food to support Shackleton's group on the final leg of their crossing. Though I have not included the story of the Ross Sea party, it is a heroic tale in its own right. The Imperial Trans-Antarctic Expedition did not officially end until the rescue of the Ross Sea party in 1917; however, the last events of the expedition that are recounted in this book took place in 1916.

I have invented none of the incidents described — all are to be found in the writings of the men who experienced them. For the men's thoughts, of course, I have had to use my imagination, but here too I was guided by what they had written. I have interwoven quotations from the men's journals, letters, memoirs, and books with my own descriptions.

NOTES ON THE TEXT

Quotations from the men's own writings used in the poem are repeated in the endnotes, with the exact wording that appears in the original documents. Differences from these original quotations as they occur in the body of the poem represent the author's paraphrasing for stylistic reasons (such as line length and rhythm and agreement in tense with surrounding lines).

In the narrative chapters of the poem, excerpts from the men's writings are set off in quotation marks. In the men's monologues, quoted excerpts are embedded in the poem without quotation marks but are fully cited in the notes.

When one of the men quotes someone else — as when Shackleton recites lines from Robert Browning — these quotations are in italics, as are the epigraphs that precede some sections of the poem.

American standard spelling is used in the narrative chapters (e.g., "color"), and British standard (e.g., "colour") in the men's monologues. The style of McNeish's monologue reflects that of his journal, acerbic as to content and eccentric as to spelling and punctuation. In their journals the men generally wrote numbers in numeral form ("20") rather than spelling them out ("twenty"), and this practice is repeated in the monologues, as is their nearly ubiquitous use of an ampersand for the word "and." Spelling of the men's names varies from document to document and among the various accounts; the most common spellings are used here.

I found most of the excerpts from the men's writings in secondary sources, and these sources are given in the notes, following each quotation.

M. M.

WHAT THE ICE GETS

＋∼＋

...and weathered many bitter nights and days
in his deep heart at sea, while he fought only
to save his life, to bring his shipmates home.

— The Odyssey
translated by Robert Fitzgerald

＋∼＋

And God's own profound
Was above me, and round me the mountains,
And under, the sea,
And within me my heart to bear witness
What was and shall be.
Oh, heaven and the terrible crystal!
No rampart excludes
Your eye from the life to be lived
In the blue solitudes.

— *"The Englishman in Italy"*
Robert Browning

Endurance

The tree is lit up with birds.

Then the landscape makes a gesture, a hornbill
going *swoop swoop swoop* into another tree.

Or, outside my window starting every March,
spring lifts its voice, monotonous
but pretty, a robin's triolet.

It can't be the same robin all these years, but here's
the thing: *It makes no difference.* One robin
or another, this hornbill or that one, in any case
the same eternals.

They flit about the branches, incandescent or drab, elusive
or confiding. Birds told over and over.

Whereas: One human or another, this man or that,
that woman or not, makes every difference —

or so I believe. A man who was a hero

tends a squalid bar in Africa — but that comes after.
Before are other stories, stories like a flock of birds.
Snow geese billow up from the surface of a lake,
a white cloth flung out by wind.

The mind rises with them as they rise…

I. INTO THE ICE
5 December 1914–
25 February 1915

They steamed out from Grytviken from the sight
of the world, dissolving into gray sleet.
Twenty-eight men on the ship *Endurance*.
They meant to make Antarctica by Christmas,
land a shore party (dogs, sledges, six men)
to cross the continent, and claim that feat
for Britain and themselves.

           The third day out
the green sea turns abruptly indigo
and then there's ice, farther north than usual.
Ice growlers riding low under the waves
rumble against the greenheart wood that sheaths
the ship. Icebergs loom and throw the masts in
shadow. The horizon glows with iceblink
from a belt of heavy pack.

           Now it's dodge
the thick ice and muscle through loose brash.
When Worsley conns the ship he makes a game
of bash and go — run the bow up a floe
to split the ice, then ram ahead. Off watch
he climbs the rigging and rides the bucking
jibboom. That this dilly is the skipper
gives some men pause. The skipper's a worry,
the ice is a worry — and yet the Ice

is beautiful. The icebergs' caverns gleam
like jade. The floes are floating marble veined
with fine long leads of azure water. "Clouds
of vapour roll skyward from the leads each
evening as the air cools. These mists freeze and
fall in shimmering showers from the clear blue
sky — a rain of jewels tinselling the ship."
Whales fountain all around; the air's shot through
with mollymawks, petrels, albatross.
Adélie penguins semaphore their flippers
and call out to the ship's biologist:
Clark! Clark! Clark! And light, light most of all, light
through all the watches. At midnight the sun
scrapes the horizon and sets it ablaze,
paves the floes gold and water copper-green.

"I think for scenery," writes Orde-Lees,
"I have not seen anything to equal
that in amongst which we now find ourselves."
In amongst which — Lees fussy in grammar
as in all else. The ropes, he notes, after
raising sail, are "exceedingly dirty."

If the wind is wrong they set ice-anchor
to a floe and play football on its cold field
with oars stuck up for goalposts. If the wind
is wrong and the weather rotten "all hands
engage in rubbing shoots off our potatoes."
When the wind is right they plow the ice and ice
shoves back at them. "There was a clatter aft
and Hussey who was at the wheel explained
'the wheel spun round and flung me over
the top of it.'"

December 30
they cross the Antarctic Circle. New Year's Eve
the ship gets squeezed between two floes and heels
six degrees to port. They use an anchor
to drag one floe astern. The bergs they pass
now are solid blue, bergs true glacier-made.
They scan the horizon for dark water-sky
but mostly it's iceblink, and all the leads
point north. They make south mile by jagged mile.
January 10 the crow's nest calls land —
there's their continent if they can reach it.
They zigzag between pack ice and the sheer
ice Barrier. When gales blow up they moor
in the lee of bergs. During the night watch
on January 19, ice congeals
round the ship.

For a month they try with steam
and sail to break out. Sometimes the men climb
overboard, swing pickaxes in the ice
and pry great chunks clear of bow and rudder.
Then Worsley backs her off and rams the floe.
Once the bow rides up the ice and sticks there;
the crew go aft and sally to and fro
on the crowded deck to rock her free. Seen
from above they look demented, dashing
rail to rail with whoops of laughter. She slides
back off the pack. The pack declines to split.
They're burning up their coal supply to no
avail. Shackleton orders engines' fires
let down. They are beset.

Shackleton

Never for me the lowered Banner.
Never the last Endeavour.

A bit of a humbug. I know people think so. Wild
thought it, years ago, when he nicknamed me *The Boss* —
with no intent to flatter. To some it's all the same as
saying, *Well, he's Irish.* All right. Humbugging got me

where I am. On the troopship out to Cape Town, in March
of 1900: charmed Longstaff into an introduction to his father,
charmed the father into getting me assigned to Scott's first
South Pole run. Then humbugged funds for my own

expedition — and that's when I learned what I can do: I can
turn back. There lay the White Road to the Pole, a mere
hundred miles left to get to glory. But the road to glory led on
to our deaths. I chose not to take it. Now Scott's laid down

all that route, and won the country's adulation. What can
adulation mean to Scott now he's dead — or to those men
he took to death beside him? When Emily asked me
how I turned around, I said better a live donkey

than a dead lion. I discovered I wouldn't kill myself
or other men for my ambition. The Prize was not
a prize unless we lived to claim it. What then
did I win, that time? Least of all the Furthest South,

an ephemera: *Furthest South — So Far.* More, my life
and further chances. *We fall to rise, are baffled to fight
better.* The best of what I won out of that journey was
Frank Wild, that steady little man — sure of me since then.

Now my longing to do something singular drives me South
again. It seems I am just good as an explorer and nothing
else, meant to live life in the blue solitudes. The territory
I most wish to claim is in men's minds — how clear to me

they are, the minds of others, though I often seem a stranger
to myself, myself a country that thwarts me when I would
go forward. But to be seen in others' eyes — not
to leave for monument my body frozen in the snow,

as Scott did, but still somehow to win through to a place
of honour in the hearts of valiant men, that is my Pole.
As to my own heart — I mean this damned knot
of muscle in my chest — I fear it. At times it socks me

like a fist and nearly knocks me to my knees, or else it
drops from under me like a hanged man through the trap.
Who knows how many chances I have left. *The old trick —
Infinite passion and finite hearts that yearn.* And now

we're locked in ice. My shipmates think we'll break out
next spring and land the sledges just as planned. I must
let them think it. Here's to humbug holding up morale.
They'll know soon enough: What the Ice gets, the Ice keeps.

II. PRESSURE
16 March–19 October 1915

We must possess ourselves in patience
till the Ice opens of its own sweet will.

It is late summer, yet the temperature
skids down to minus thirty and the sea
turns to stone. The *Endurance* is bewitched;
the waves piled at her keel never break. Mock
suns and the sun are tethered in halos.
Icebergs hang in midair. Refraction hoists
them there, turns them upside down, draws them up
as wavering spires "that spread out till they meet,
forming long, beautiful phantom snow-cliffs
washed at their bases by the waters
of illusion." The continent dissolves
and floats above the sea in cloudy skeins.
Auroras unfurl and flicker green or
sluice upward in crimson and purple flames.
The air's so clear it's as if there is no
air, all sense of distance lost: they set out
to explore a nearby berg, sledge all day
and never get close. The sun subsides toward
the horizon, until one evening when
it seems to set and rise three times before
it founders into night. Then night becomes
a season, scoured by a never-setting
moon that drifts round like an iceberg through
the stars.

Against this sorcery and the cold
the Boss exerts the ordinary: Their minds
must stay unfrozen and undark. Routine
and food and work are laid on as a poultice
over fear, and the men are not afraid.
The biologist studies diatoms
and penguins; the geologist makes do
with pebbles from the penguins' stomachs;
the rest hunt the birds for food and fuel.
An emperor penguin Kerr pursues gets
the best of him, knocks him sprawling and stands
on his chest till Cheetham chases it off.
Penguins, seals, dogs, and men: in all that scape
of ice there's nothing else alive. They long
for life's hubbub and find it in the dogs,
who yip, bay, and tussle with one another
and the crew. The bitch Sally has a litter
and great rawboned Crean nursemaids the pups.
When the dogs get into fights Macklin wades in
and wallops both contestants with his fist.
Disputes among the men are put to Wild.
"He is tremendously approachable,
always outstandingly ready to help
in every way." "A wonderful foil
to the Boss's Irish temperament."

Macklin runs his dog team in the moonlight
and Cheetham rides along. "I say, Doctor.
Don't you think we are better off than the King?
I'm happy and you're happy and here we are
sitting on a sledge driving smoothly home
and looking at the wonders of the World;
it goes into your soul, like, don't it Doctor?"
Lees rides his bicycle out on the Ice,

gets lost, has to be retrieved, gets scolded
by the Boss. "No one knows how much it means
to me, having a bicycle and a place
to ride it, however rough the going."
And Hurley — "Hurley is a warrior
with the camera," "taking pictures
by the fathom, with cheerful Australian
profanity." He hauls his equipment
to the crow's nest and films the crew playing
hockey on the floes. When daylight returns
he hikes across the Ice to photograph
ice flowers forming in the leads, "a field
of pink carnations." And he wires up
twenty flashes around the ship to sear
this image on a plate: the *Endurance*
rises into the black cathedral vault
of polar night, her masts and all her rigging
white with frost. Her stark form makes the darkness
visible. She looks a lovely ghost.

What threatens her is Pressure, the Ice driven
against her keel by force of far-off gales.
They can see the Pressure coming for miles:
The ice field is riven into blocks that
raft up in jumbled heaps; the heaps roar
forward in a line of pressure ridges.
Frost-smoke cloaks the world behind a violet
pall, fuming out where cracks lay water bare.
If it's dark or they're below decks, they know
when Pressure's going to hit them by the sounds:
"an enormous train with squeaky axles,
mingled with the sound of steamer whistles
and groans of souls in torment." One day

"a terrible noise, like a thousand guns
going off" — Pressure squeezes the *Endurance*
up out of the Ice and she heels over
almost on her beam-ends, thirty degrees
to port. Pandemonium. Dogs are thrown
howling from their kennels, crates somersault
from one bulwark to the other. The men
scuttle about the ship to find how badly
she's been hurt, searching her for leaks or fires.

After nightfall the Ice lets go its grip.
Endurance rights herself and settles back
in her narrow slip of water; the crew
return to usual shipboard routine.
But Shackleton now confides to Worsley
what he and Wild already know: "The ship
can't live in this, Skipper. What the Ice gets
the Ice keeps."

        Still, the men don't need to see,
just yet, what is coming. They stage a burlesque
to allay their boredom. Some of the men
shave their beards to play the roles of women —
Worsley calls this heroic; most of them
have grown their beards like fur against the cold.
Marston bats his eyelashes against two
beefy cheeks, a rather fantastical
woman, but women here are fantasies
in any case. (Shackleton keeps, for whimsy,
a letter received from three girls asking
to be taken on as members of the crew:
"We do not see why men should have all
the glory and women none, when there are

women just as brave and capable
as men.") The evening's entertainment ends
as always, with a toast: "To our wives and
sweethearts. May they never meet."

Crean. Night Watch

What would make Crean blush
would make a butcher's dog drop its bone.

Coming back from Captain Scott's
last voyage, well, we sailed
into Oamaru in dead of night
and stood off till dawn, hailed

though we were by the lighthouse — *What ship?*
What ship? — wanting to prevent
the news from getting out till the families
could be cabled, as was only decent.

A funeral ship we were, that time.
Nor will I forget the sight
of what we found inside that tent.
Yet back I've come in spite

of all. One thing, I'd like to stand
at the Pole. I was that close
I could have shouted at it, and when
Scott turned us back and chose

the other team for the last push,
I'm not ashamed to say
it was a blow brought me to tears.
We watched them march away

and thought them a sure bet. And so
they were — to reach the Pole.
It's the coming home was more than they
could do, God rest their souls.

Sledging up the Beardmore Glacier,
I once saw the team ahead
lifted by mirage, their doubles hung
in air above their heads

as if the Ice breathed out a mirror.
In the Ice you see your mates
for what they're worth — see yourself,
what's more, and love or hate

what shows there. I knew a man
came South with brown eyes
and went back home with blue ones,
their colour frozen by the Ice.

More than how you look, 'tis what
you see that changes most.
The first time I saw trees again,
they looked to me like green ghosts.

III. WHAT THE ICE GETS
23–29 October 1915

Out of whose womb came the ice?
And the hoary frost of heaven, who hath gendered it?
The waters are hid as with a stone,
And the face of the deep is frozen.

Two floes catch hold of the ship, one to port,
the other starboard. A third floe grinding aft
tears out her sternpost. The salt sea pours in.
McNeish wades into the engine room
and starts a cofferdam to stanch the bleeding.
Behind him Rickinson and Kerr shovel
fuel into the engines — coal, blubber, wood —
anything to get her fires up and drive
the steam pumps. But the steam pumps can't keep pace
and the hand pumps are choked with ice. Worsley,
Greenstreet, and Hudson clamber below decks
to clear them, scrambling through darkness over
lurching coal. Ice-cold water surges round
their legs, and in their ears explodes a din
of cracking beams, like rifle shots. The men
go on watch and watch, four hours at the pumps
or swinging pickaxes to break the Ice
that grips her keel. Four hours uneasy rest,
then back to pumps and axes. "Every muscle
aches, revolting at the agony of toil."
For three days they keep at it with scant sleep.
McNeish still works in water to his waist,

he and Hurley caulking the dam with strips
of blanket. The engineers keep steam up,
though beside them the thick bulkheads heave in
and out as the Ice shifts, "giving the awful
impression that the ship gasps for breath."
The air resounds with shrieks of rending wood,
whinging yowls of dogs and roaring Pressure.
Eight emperor penguins approach the ship,
stretch their throats and keen like banshees. McLeod,
who's refused to eat penguin meat because
they are drowned sailors' souls, turns to Macklin:
"Hear that? We'll none of us get home again."
Shackleton gropes up the deck and sees how
the ship's been bent like a bow in the rack
of ice. He orders stores and boats lowered
to the floes. Worsley tears out charts and maps
from the ship's books, choosing every landfall
they might need to reach, or could. Green — well Green's
a cook, so he cooks dinner. Then the fires
are all let down so the engines won't blow
when the sea floods in. Some men make a chute
of canvas and toss the dogs into it
to slide them to the Ice. Wild picks his way
fore and aft, finding the men off-watch who've
dropped asleep exhausted. "She's going, boys.
It's time to get off." The decks break upward
as they climb overboard. Her stretched rigging
sings in the wind. Higher and higher notes.

On the floe they try to sleep. But all night
"you hear the Ice being ground into her.
You almost feel it is your own ribs
being crushed. It seems the end of everything."
Eerie groans and shouts, jigs, ululations

from a mosque, keenings, long chords too low
to hear but that shake the heart from its chest
like leaves out of a tree — grisly music
wrung from the ship by the Ice that breaks her.
The Boss and Wild stand on watch while the rest
lie in their tents. They jury-rig a stove
and in the morning boil up hot milk
for all hands. All hands accept without remark.
Wild plants a fist on either hip and says,
"If any of you gentlemen also
wants his boots blacked, kindly leave them outside
your doors."

      Nearby the *Endurance* lies
mangled in the Ice, all her fine bones
broken. White shards driven through her sides
hold her up, "sullen dark against the sky."
Shackleton musters the crew. "Well, boys. Ship
and stores have gone. So now we'll go home."
Crean takes the youngest pups and the ship's cat
behind a hummock of ice and shoots them.
The food won't stretch past working dogs and men.

McNeish & Hurley

A man must shape himself to a new mark
directly the old one goes to ground.

Well 'tis all up with the ship the Ice has cut clean
Through her & next thing the Boss sends Mr Crean

To do away with the cat as the Boss says we can keep
But two pounds each besides our clothes. He makes a heap

Of his own things & shows us gold coins in his palm
Then throws them down & tears the 23rd Psalm

Out of his Bible & lays the Bible on the Ice to make
His point. Well I guess each man is going to take

What he values most & I for one have wrapt my Bible
With fotos of my Loved ones as we're liable

To need prayers as much as food from what I see.
The cat was that fond of me they called her Mrs Chippy.

> *Our scene is as strange as a nightmare. The wardroom clock*
> *kept ticking in its ordinary way last night while great ice blocks*
>
> *ground the ship like millstones. Now this morning we've woken*
> *to a tumult of lifted slabs in all directions, the whole landscape broken*
>
> *as if Creation were a failure and had to be done over. So it's little matter*
> *that I've got to cull my negatives, choose out my best work and shatter*

all the rest against temptation to keep more than my share. Circumstance
is a ruthless editor. This floe won't last forever; then we must chance

the boats and open ocean, three boats to carry all the party and our gear.
So: here's our world last March, clouds purling and unpurling above sheer

cliffs of Rampart Berg. Smash it goes, and adds its little part to the vast
cullet of ice. The upturned floes are lit through like thick blue glass.

I'm to fix up sledges for the boats so I'm at pulling
Nails out of what parts of the ship is still showing

Above the Ice. The new nails is all in boxes drownd
In her hold with most of my tools but I've found

My hammer adze chisel & a saw & since nails is nails
I'll do all right. I told the Boss there's timber & sails

Enough to salvage that I could build a sloop for all
The party but he says no. He says we're going to haul

The boats & gear over the Ice to get to land, Well he can
Say so but I have my doubts. I think if we go & bang

The boats over this rough business they won't be fit
To carry feathers much less us & then we'll be in for it

If his plan don't work. But the good news is I chopped
A hole in the ship's deck & crates of stores popped

Right up like corks. Some like the walnuts not much
Use but plenty else we'll be glad of flour & such.

I started the day as trip's photographer and ended handyman.
I filmed the masts breaking away, then I sealed the film in cans

and threw away all my equipment, keeping just a pocket camera
with three rolls of film for my "two pounds." So ends that era.

Now I'm at work making a decent blubber-stove from the ship's
ash chute. Having nothing but Chippy's blunt flat chisel to chip

two fifteen-inch holes in the steel makes for a somewhat arduous
undertaking. I've nicked myself a dozen times and used strenuous

language but I have high hopes for the outcome. I have my eye
on some timbers to floor the tents with, which will keep us dry

instead of lying on the ice. And I'm certain I can build a portable
boat-stove from the ash bucket. So it seems I'm still employable,

cameras or no. Tonight Sir E. is reciting Browning in our tent
so I'll fire Keats across his bow — aren't we two proper, grimy gents?

We've not had one Sunday service since we sailed out on this voyage
So our dismal luck is no surprise & I wonder with the wreckage
Of the ship & ship's routine how long till they all turns savage?

IV. OCEAN CAMP
30 October–27 December 1915

Yes, but we are not going to let the Ice get us.

At first they bustle about, inventing
comfort. Wild with his dog team drags the wheel-
house off the ship; it becomes the kitchen
and camp library. Salvaged volumes of
Encyclopædia Britannica
sit on packing-crate shelves, borrowed at night
for reading — or the less edifying
pages burned to eke out the match supply.
Marston turns from ship's artist to cobbler
and resoles all their boots. He gives McNeish
his oil paints to caulk the boats and uses
what's left to paint names the Boss has chosen
on their bows: *Stancomb Wills, Dudley Docker,*
James Caird — the voyage's chief financiers.
Hurley studies the ship's compass binnacle
and it's reborn as bilge pump for the *Caird.*
They hammer together a lookout tower
and run up the Royal Thames Yacht Club flag.
Shackleton dons Worsley's dress uniform —
the cocked hat and white boat-cloak have floated
somehow from the hold. He thrusts a shovel
in his belt for sword and conducts a mock
inspection; Hussey attends with spade-at-arms.
Greenstreet and Macklin hop on a small floe
and punt up and down a lead with ski poles.

"It is just like school days over again,
and very jolly, too — for the time being."

On November 21 the Boss calls
from the lookout, "Boys! The ship! She's sinking."
The Pressure has relaxed; the spears of ice
on which she hangs give way and she goes down
by the head. Her stern rises, shudders, hangs
a moment — slides away. The water gapes
where she had been. The landscape is bereft
of all but their makeshift camp and miles of ice.
"Without her our destitution seems more
emphasized." "We are now very lonely."

Drift of the pack had been bearing them north
toward Paulet Island, the nearest landfall.
They have consoled themselves with an idea
of riding their snug floe like a magic
carpet till it fetched up on the island,
where lies a hut of stores from a prior
expedition. But now the wind shifts north-
northwest and blows a thaw. The ice beneath
their camp turns rotten, the pack gnaws their floe
around its edges and they walk and sleep
in slush. Shackleton regards them, hearing
cheerfulness stretched thin as hope recedes
with Paulet Island. He decides: if Hope
cannot sit still, it can be hauled.

                              They load
sledges and boats with stores and their allowance
of gear, plus some dispensations — Hussey's
banjo, Hurley's saved negatives, ship's log.
The dog teams pull out first. Where ice ridges

can't be skirted they must hack a pathway
for the boats. Eighteen men in harness haul
the boats in relays. Each boat weighs a ton.
Every time they stop, the sledge runners freeze
to the ice and the men must throw themselves
against their traces half a dozen times
to jerk free. They drag one boat a hundred yards,
then walk back and hitch up to the next one.
They make two crawling miles each day, or less,
sinking to knees or hips in swampy snow.
Two hundred miles stretch ahead to Paulet.
The fifth day McNeish throws his harness down
and won't budge, and the others stand around
to see what the Boss will do. The Boss reads
Ship's Articles aloud: "The Crew agree
to be obedient to lawful commands."
He tells McNeish: March or be shot. Then walks
away. McNeish takes up his trace without
a word. The next day they pull five hours
to make 200 yards, one ridge after
another to be axed down, the men half
wading in soft ice. Shackleton and Wild
climb a small berg and scan the view ahead:
a cataclysm of broken ice
crisscrossed with leads. It can't be done.

V.   WAITING WAITING WAITING
31 December 1915–8 April 1916

All around us we have day after day the same
unbroken whiteness unrelieved by anything at all.

"Nothing to do, nowhere to walk, no change
in surroundings, food or anything. God
send us open water soon or we shall
go balmy." Their fate all lies with the Wind,
witless and indifferent. It may scud them
nearer land. It may open the Ice and let
them launch the boats. Or else it will sweep them
out to sea in close pack — *Nothing to do* —
no open water and the floe ground down
to bits beneath their feet. *Nowhere to walk.*
"A bug on a single molecule
in a gale of wind would have the same chance."

"Nothing to do, see or say. The worst thing
is having to kill time." To stay alive
they have to slaughter all the life they see
for food and fuel. Seals. Penguins. They wake
one day to a great flock of Adélies
on the floe, "making quaint noises like men
talking in deep tones." The men snatch up clubs
and knives. In three days they kill six hundred.
All they have to eat is death and not enough
of that. "Stewed penguin heart, liver, eyes, tongues,
toes & God knows what else." *No change of food.*

At last they kill the dogs. "The duty falls
upon me, the worst job I ever had
in my life." Wild and Macklin lead each dog
behind a hummock. Wild sits the dog down
and cups its muzzle in his palm. The dog
looks at his face, curious. *The worst thing.*
Wild puts the revolver to its head. Macklin
drags the body off. He carried the dog Grus
in his pocket as a pup, "with only
his nose peeping out and getting covered
with frost." Macklin skins out Grus's body.
Crean butchers his dog Nelson and visits
the tents. "I've brought a bit of Nelson for
you to try."

        Hunger makes them cold. They walk
round and round the floe at night to get warm
enough to sleep. The floe was once a mile
across but it shrinks day by day. *Nowhere
to walk.* One of the Able-Bodied sailors
"wraps copper wire around his belly and
thinks he is going to walk home." *God send
open water soon or we shall go balmy.*

Nothing to do, see or say. Hussey plays
his banjo less and less, as "his 6 tunes
is heartbreaking." Worsley dreams a headline
in the *Daily Mail*: "Compulsory Trans
Antarctic Expedition." Hurley dreams
of trying to drown squirming dogs who turn
to seals "and regard me with gummy eyes."
Shackleton starts up from nightmares every
night. "I long for some rest, free from thought."
"I long for a place where the direction
of the wind doesn't mean a Tinker's cuss."

The sun lets down its pale net through a hole
chopped in the clouds. The clouds are floes, close-packed
or rifted with blue leads. In the liquid
cold beneath them the men feel that they
are drowning. *God send us open water*
soon or we shall go balmy. They call this
Patience Camp. Not patience but apathy
possesses them. All but Wild. He turns up
at the tent assigned to night watch, bringing
a match from scant supplies to light their pipes,
then spins them bawdy yarns that make them laugh.
Misery can't change him nor despair find
any purchase.

        Worsley climbs a small berg
every day and scans the Ice for land. Bergs
in shadow look like land. Clouds and fogbanks
appear as land. *No change in surroundings.*
He sights James Ross Island — "He says he has
seen it but we know him to be a liar."
Cape pigeons fly overhead. Terns. Petrels.
Worsley says they signify open water
close by. *But we know him to be a liar.*
"Pray God we may find a landing." "Please God
we will soon get ashore." *God send open*
water soon. McNeish recaulks the boats
with blood of seals. *No change no change no change.*

Orde-Lees

Well, Old Lady. We've got it in the neck this time, haven't we?

I seem to be a person to whom nicknames & arguments
adhere. Old Lady (that's for my being finical).
Man of Action (a comment
on my propensity to shirk). The Colonel
(they think I put on airs from being in the Service).
Belly Burglar, now that Sir Ernest

has placed me in charge of stores — because I'm finical! And here's
a paradox: stores dwindle but my task increases
in difficulty. My fears
irritate Sir Ernest, who never ceases
to insist we put forward an optimistic view.
This is for benefit of the crew —

Sir Ernest thinks if we lay in seal & penguin meat in excess
of present needs, they'll panic at the thought of winter
on the Ice. So one's prowess
at hunting is a vice that's seen to hinder
morale rather than help! My companions seem to live
in the moment; that one can't help give

thought to the future makes one an irritant. In January
I brought in a quantity of meat by accident.
I was out hunting on ski —
illicitly! — when a sea leopard, intent
on hunting *me*, lunged onto the floe, thinking I was
a wondrously large penguin or else

a strangely upright seal. I yelled — my pursuer gaining fast
on me — and Wild ran out with his rifle, drew the beast
to himself & at the last
instant shot it, all the while adding a feast
of gaudily coloured nicknames to one's collection.
So that provided us with rations

for a time. We've used up the last of the cocoa, the last flour;
we've reached the end of bacon, cheese, coffee, tea. It feels
as if hunger will devour
us, having so little else to feed on. Meals
consist of: dog pemmican & a lump of sugar
for breakfast (there's too little blubber

left for making hot milk); one hot meal of penguin or seal hoosh;
the third meal is three lumps of sugar & one biscuit.
Stores left behind in our push
for land lie across broken ice; we'd risk it
to retrieve them but Sir Ernest forbids us, for fear
those who went would get stranded. Near-

starvation seems less a horror to him than splitting the party.
He is at ease only with us all in his direct care.
While on a hunting sortie
yesterday I fainted — One's hoarding a share
of one's rations against a fear of future need may
be unwise, as one is hungrier day

to day than one's less provident fellows. However, last night
nausea woke me — it can hardly be indigestion
with so little to digest! Might
I be sea-sick from nearby open ocean
heaving our floe? Worsley also thinks he feels some swells;
Sir Ernest orders boat-loading drills.

VI. OPEN WATER
9–15 April 1916

The floe rises to the swell, cracks, then cracks
again. The men strike camp and load the boats.
Where Shackleton's tent once stood he can see
the image of his sleeping body, melted
in the floe. Then the image breaks in two.
They launch the boats.

                    They're barely under way
when two tumbling walls of ice sweep toward them,
borne on tidal rips. If they're caught between,
they'll be buried. The men at oars lay back
hard; the other men chant *stroke!…stroke!…stroke!*
and stamp their feet in rhythm. Seabirds whirl
around them and shower them with droppings;
the rowers duck their heads and pull for all
their lives. The ice-swells clash together
just behind the boats. They row on through brash,
and camp at dusk on a sturdy-seeming
floe. Shackleton can't sleep but paces up
and down the ice. At midnight the floe splits
beneath a tent, dropping How and Holness
in the sea. How kicks free of his fur bag
and scrambles clear. Shackleton grabs Holness
and heaves sodden man and bag onto the ice,
and as he does, the floe's broken halves crash
shut again. The men walk Holness round

in circles until dawn so he won't freeze
to death. The next day delirious zig-
zagging through the pack brings them to the gray
and open sea. They hoist sail for a dash
toward Clarence Island but the *Stancomb Wills*
hasn't got the canvas and lags so far
behind, the *Docker* comes about and takes
the *Wills* in tow. They fight through heavy chop
and freezing spray, the boats growing sluggish
as they're sheathed in ice. From the *Caird*, the Boss
waves them toward the pack: it's get some shelter
or be swamped. They haul up on a low berg
for the night

                     and wake under siege. Tall swells
of rolling ice snarl forward out of mist
and avalanche against their berg. Grandeur
inescapable. The berg lurches, yaws,
threatens to capsize. Pieces shear away
with deafening shrieks. They can't take to the boats
and soon there will be no place left to stand.
They try to joke about their peril, fall
silent, try writing in their diaries
and fail. Some hear lines of poems reeling
through their heads. *I never saw, nor shall see,*
here or elsewhere, till I die...I never saw,
nor shall see, here or elsewhere — A slim lane
of water opens; they throw the boats pell-
mell off the berg, leap in and row like hell.

Shackleton vows he'll never risk a camp
on ice again. That night, they tie the boats
together and hunker down inside them.
"Ghostly shadows of silver petrels flash
close to us. Snow-showers fall silently

on the sea, laying a thin shroud of white
over our bodies." Killer whales roll up
from the murk beneath the boats, hissing steam,
eye-level with the men, monstrous. The men
can't sleep for fright and cold. Hudson cries out —
"A light! I see a light!" There's nothing there.

The next day's bright and bitter. Blown spray turns
to ice on their Burberrys; when they row
the ice shatters and they look like statues
breaking into painful life. Their hands slip
on the iced-up oar looms and raise blisters,
then the fluid in the blisters freezes
to gravel in their palms. Night brings no
relief, no chance to cook, no sleep. They start
to the oars when a vast berg advances
on them "but this resolves into a cloud
lit by the rising moon." At dawn the wind
hauls round and they run before it, the *Wills*
towed behind the *Caird*. They're tormented now
by thirst, drenching seas, seasickness, frostbite,
dysentery. They hang over the gunwales
to shit and vomit. They chew raw seal meat
to wet their throats with blood. The *Docker*'s crew
console themselves with violent cursing, curse
the weather, curse the boat, curse rotten luck.
Open water — bloody hell! Marston sits
in the bow and bellows songs: *Twankedil-*
lo, twankedillo, and my roaring pair
of bagpipes. When Stephenson's not rowing
he covers his face and weeps.

                    The Boss fears
some of them won't last the night, but they do.
A yellow seam opens in the darkness

and through it pours a sunrise of such glory
it lifts them like some comfort of the flesh.
Out of a pink mist on the horizon
Elephant Island takes shape, forty miles
north, right where Worsley said it was. The men
have learned what the Skipper's good for — put him
in a boat and he's a genius. He's gone
three days without sleeping to chart their course.
Refuge is in sight and they pull for it
hard, yet they seem to stand still on the waves,
beaten back by an offshore wind that blows
a gale by nightfall. If they miss this land
in the darkness, beyond it lies — Nothing.
It's make landfall or die. Wild steers by blink
of moonlight on the island's glaciers, hunched
at the *Caird*'s tiller now for days, "always
the same confident blue-eyed little man,
looking to the day ahead." The Boss sits
beside him with his hand on the painter
of the *Wills* — If they lose her, she'll be lost
for good. The slender line yanks tight and slack,
tight and slack, weighted with ice that threatens
to fray it apart. They can't see the waves
that slam them, can't see the *Wills*; fog obscures
the guiding moon. The *Docker* vanishes
in the storm. Shackleton signals, shining
a candle on his sail, but gets no answer.
It is "a stern night," "the worst night I have
ever known." Half the men are catatonic
with despair. "Think we are getting out
to sea and lost."

They wait for light to show
unbounded ocean, death's gray face. "Dawn

at last — and find ourselves bang in front of land."
"It is the eastern tip of the island
which we have only just managed to grasp."
The *Docker* heaves into view and they run
the boats onto a rocky beach. Some men
fling themselves on the ground and roll about
or pile rocks on their bodies. One man hacks
ten seals to death, crazed by too many days
of anguish. Shackleton's face is haggard,
his voice gone. "Only little Frankie Wild
looks something like his normal self." They eat
and drink and sleep, stand watch and sleep and eat.
"How delicious to wake in one's sleep
and listen to the chanting of penguins
mingled with music of the sea." The surf
elides in and out of shingle, the first
sounds of land they've heard in sixteen months.

Worsley

*A rather wild, excitable, hare-brained, half grown up
kind of customer quite incapable of responsible action.*

Oh the pleasures of Elephant Island. Soon after we retired to our tents
an uncouth wind cuffed them flat, so we've accommodated ourselves
to the quaint circumstance of lying with sharp rocks probing our backs
and wet canvas on our faces. With the storm screaming around us the effect
is of sleeping on a train track under ghostly trains — trains of snow. Normal
persons would not find this much like the Riviera but we are quite content,
each wrapped in his own thoughts as cosily as in his bag, enjoying
the luxury of reminiscence, now every instant isn't a crisis of mortal danger.

We float off to sleep,
get jabbed awake by an ill-mannered rock,
enjoy life, seeing that the rocks at least will not melt or drift with the wind,
rehearse a snippet or two of past events,
and float off again…

How I came to be known as Wuzzles: The fact is
when a ship is stuck fast in ice like a plum in a plum-cake,
her skipper becomes a Vestigial Person whom no one
quite knows what to do with, including himself. So Himself,
having come for adventure, found other ways of having it.
Such as shouting, "Tally-ho!" and dashing out
onto the floe in a state of nature for a snow bath.
Poor Crean catching sight of me naked on the Ice
thought I'd "gone wrong in the napper." That
and other incidents had my shipmates regarding me
as a sort of circus animal, to be watched closely —
for amusement but also should he go off on a rampage.

Oh but the sky — the sky was not gripped by ice but sailed
in utter freedom, the stars streaming in great currents overhead
through the winter night. In summer the white ice was a canvas
and the sky painted upon it the purest colours I have ever seen.

One night I took a longitude by Mercury, for swank.

I notice I can't distinguish lulls
in the storm from the internal
lull of falling asleep...

After our poor gallant ship went down — still the one event of all
our tribulations I cannot find the heart to joke about — the men never
knew it, but once the sledges pulled out for Paulet Island, Shackleton
sent me back to Ocean Camp to leave a note in a sealed bottle:
        Endurance *crushed and abandoned in 69°5' S. and 51°35' W.*
        All hands proceeding to the westward. All well. December 23rd, 1915.
— a kind of will and testament of the expedition. It would have frightened
some of them to know the Boss had left such a message — thinking
a bottle in the ocean had more chance than we did of being found.

When the ship's sturdy reality was
snug about us, we had enjoyed the whimsies of the Ice —
the fantastical berg castles, the ice hummocks sculpted
into such likenesses of cities it would not have shocked us
to be hailed by voices.

But when we came to live
in that white city we turned to dream-men,
drifting in a ghost of the world and
longing for its solid flesh —
real stones, real streets, real
anything...

How grim it was, landing here, to see grown men
play with stones like children — shambling,
dirty, bearded, weeping children.

This is a refuge, but not rescue. No ships come here, no ships will ever
come here. Someone's going to have to sail for help. It's not a pretty prospect
in such savage weather. Trying to land, we thought we'd be driven
on the rocks. I've never seen such winds, plummeting down the cliffs like
cataracts — the gusts fell on us from above and smashed the waves to pieces.
We rowed like men possessed; me swearing we would "get to wind'ard or sink
the bitch." We got to wind'ard. The men think I can work miracles
with a boat, navigate by half a glimpse of sun, or when the sun fails
read the birds to find my way to land —

and all right, snow petrels do mean pack ice
fulmars, open ocean
and grey petrels signal islands —

and Crean keeps telling me
I was never born to be drowned,
though for *hanged* he gives no guarantees.

But my God. South Georgia Island is our only chance and it's a tiny morsel
eight hundred miles away.

VII. THE *James Caird*
24 April—9 May 1916

Superhuman effort isn't worth a damn
unless it achieves results.

This is what they longed for, all those white months
on the Ice, all those days in the misery
of the boats. Land, solid land, rooted fast
to the floor of the world and not adrift.
The object of their ardent dreams is bleak
and brutal. Elephant Island assails
them with an unrelenting wind so fierce
it knocks them off their feet. Blocks of ice hurtle
through the air, their mitts are torn off their hands,
their sleeping bags fill with snow. Wild drags
them bodily from the tents' ruins, "none
too gently either" — They must kill penguins
or go hungry, stay in motion or go
under. In appalling cold "only warmth
of the dead penguins' bodies saves our hands."

They had thought to wait till spring, then sail on
to Deception Island where whalers come.
But they can't withstand this, some of them, can't
bear the thought of enduring here for months.
Shackleton's got somehow to give them hope.
He tells them he's going to sail for rescue
in the *Caird*. The night before they set out,
Worsley considers his shipmates, filthy

tattered men in tattered clothes, branded with
the ashy brands of frostbite. "A series
of pictures haunts me — of what will become
of these men if we should fail. I feel I
cannot get my fill of gazing at them."

Six men are going to undertake the voyage
in the *Caird*. Shackleton and Worsley. Crean.
Chippy McNeish. Vincent, demoted months
ago from bos'n, for bullying the men
(best get him where he'll do less harm). Timmy
McCarty, ox-built and cheerful. Wild stays
behind, in charge of all the rest. The Boss
leaves with him a letter. "I have every
confidence in you and always have had.
May God prosper your work and your life.
You can convey my love to my people."

Day One. They launch the *Caird* through heavy surf,
sent off with "three squawky cheers from the men
and penguins." Offshore they pick their way through
a jostling drove of ice. Worsley's thoughts burst
out in manic whimsy — the woeful image
of those scarecrows falling astern under
grim scarps needs driving off. "Castles,
towers, and churches sway unsteadily
around us. Swans of weird shape peck our planks,
a gondola steered by a giraffe runs
foul of us, which much amuses a duck
sitting on a crocodile's head...." All night
he and Shackleton steer north by the stars.

Day Two. Day Three. Day Four. The wind hauls south
and blows a gale. They're shipping seas every

several minutes. They bail and pump through watch
and watch and still hear water sloshing through
the ballast. There's no other sound but wind
in the shrouds, no sight to see but gray, gray
seas and spray, gray sodden clouds. Men and gear
are soaked and soaked for good. The taste of salt
never leaves their mouths.

> *Day Five, Day Six.* Seas
rise astern twice as tall as the boat is
long, so tall the sails go dead in the troughs
between — Cape Horn rollers. Each precipice
plunges forward, looking sure to bury
them, but hoists the *Caird* up to its hissing
summit. There's a dizzying glimpse of more
rollers to the horizons, then they slide
backward down the far slope. The boat is rigged
with a mizzen, lugsail, and jib — three "large
handkerchiefs" against the Southern Ocean —
and she gripes to windward. The helmsman fights
the rudder to hold her off the wind while
the others bail the ocean overboard.

Day Seven & *Day Eight.* The gale rises
to such screaming pitch they've got to heave to,
throw out sea anchor and hunker below
the canvas decking. At first water pours
as always down their necks, but then it slows,
trickles, stops. Ice has sealed the boat. To have
one misery relent amounts almost
to coziness. They fall asleep

> and wake
uneasy. Where before the boat chopped waves

like an ax, now she wallows. Ice a foot
thick on her deck is sinking her. In turns
they slither out on hands and knees to club
ice off. Three times she ices up, three times
they clear her. *Day Nine* a lump of ice
saws through the anchor's rope. She slews broadside
to the wind till they wrestle the jib up.
The shrinking span of daylight lifts the gloom
a fraction and falls back into darkness.
Shackleton sees a pale rift in the night
and thinks *clear sky at last* — but it's the crest
of a leviathan wave. It thunders
down on them and pours a thrashing torrent
into the boat — they have foundered, they are
drowning — they are just afloat and bailing
with cups, hands, anything, *get her empty
or we're done for.* When they've done it the gale

has dropped, spent as they are spent. *Days Ten &
Eleven,* the sun's out, Old Jamaica
as friendly as you please. They strew their clothes
and bags on the rigging to dry, the bags
half rotted. They pitch the slimiest two
overboard. The Boss ribs Crean — "Go to sleep
Crean and don't be clucking like an old hen" —
and Crean in turn chaffs Worsley with *Skipper,
darlin'.* They gurgle with laughter through lips
too cracked for grinning. The shouldering swells
drive them on, eighty, ninety miles a day.

Day Twelve, Day Thirteen. So close now, so close,
and worry creeps back. Soon they'll know whether
it's all a failure and they've missed the jot
of land that is their one hope. A bobtailed

seabird they haven't seen before pesters
the boat, "always in a fussy, bustling
state," Orde-Lees haunting them in bird-form.
Shackleton flails at it and swears, irate
out of all proportion, the only glimpse
the men get of what's pent up behind his
bullish coolness. The weight of all their lives.

Day Fourteen. Somehow Worsley's got to get
a sighting of the sun and fix their course.
He kneels on a thwart, gripped by McCarty
and Vincent so he's not flung overboard.
The sun's a vague blot in fog. He guesses
at its center through the sextant, brings it
down to a guessed horizon — "the boat jump-
ing like a flea" — and snaps the altitude.
Then he peels apart the soggy pages
of his navigation books and works out
a guess at where they are. If his guesses
are wrong the Atlantic will swallow them.

Day Fifteen. A streamer of kelp floats past
and then shags come flying, "a guarantee
you are within fifteen miles of land." They
try to bore their eyes through the mist, they must
be close, must be. The morning passes, noon
comes and goes, then McCarty shouts out, *Land!*
Land O! The fog shreds on a peak, they all
see it: South Georgia, Worsley's reckoning
dead on. They can just make out tussock grass
and moss, tender barely remembered green.
Dusk is falling. They stand off. Worsley scans
a livid sky — dirty weather's coming
hard at them.

The wind rises in the night
to eighty knots. Then they hear a worse sound
growing below its screeches — the bass note
of surf pounding a lee shore. If they can't
claw off they'll be dashed to pieces. Worsley
and Crean crawl on their bellies to the mast
to shift sail. It takes an hour. The *Caird* slams
into waves and her planks open, spurting
water. They bail death overboard, praying
for sea room, sea room or a change of wind.
"Night wears on. Very tired. Gale & sea
too much for us. We long for day." Dawn shows
them not South Georgia Island but the coast
of the next world. They can't beat back upwind
against this storm; it hurls them toward the cliffs.
It is *Day Sixteen* since setting out. Their goal
rushes at them. They no longer believe
they will get there as living men.

VIII. ELEPHANT ISLAND
24 April–29 August 1916

*Miss Sir E. very much. We expect
relief in about a fortnight.*

Day One. Water seethes to and fro; the bay's
a mess of surf and ice. Sopping men
launch the *Caird*. *How we shall count the days.*

In Hurley's photograph the horizon's
over their heads. They stand before the ocean
as before a wall. Waving. Their comrades
sail over its top. "That's the last of them,"
a man mutters, and Wild for once loses
patience and rounds on him "with real lower
deck language." He looks at the others, sees
some of them in tears, and sets them to work.
Waiting is their true task, but they must seem
to be doing something else. Their suitors
are despair in all its guises, watching
them with gimlet eyes. They need some shelter.
For tonight they drag the *Wills* up the spit
to a deserted rookery — knowing
penguins won't nest within reach of waves — up-
end the boat, crawl into the reek beneath,
and there begin to heft time from present
into past. A shivering measure of sleep:
Done. The bitter parcel of rising: Done.

Wind screams oaths and snow and rends the bay.
In this fury they are to do their part
toward their rescue: survive till comes the day.

They build a hut: lug rocks for walls and lash
the boats across for roof. Hurley fashions —
of course he does — a stove from an oil drum.
Kerr discerns a chimney in the lining
of a biscuit case. So there's your kitchen.
Sometimes wind blows blubber smoke backward down
the biscuit tin and fumigates the place.
The boat thwarts become a loft for sleeping.
They dub their hut the Snuggery and chink
its walls with snow to keep out snow. Won't Sir E.
admire what's been done, when he returns.

A fortnight passes. Now they sketch the bay
with relief ships — scribble of smoke or mast's
resolving line. Any day now. Any day.

Orde-Lees and Wild argue over food.
Lees wants to stockpile every penguin or
seal that comes ashore. Wild thinks the crew will
see in each body flung on the cooling
mound another day they'll be stranded here.
Lees persists. Wild threatens to shoot him
if he can't keep his tongue between his teeth.
Lees retires to his journal where he frets
at Wild's improvidence. Wild is frugal
with hope — more than scurvy or starvation
he fears their coming to the end of hope.

A white rind of pack ice jackets the bay.
No relief ship could break through ice this thick.
There's no point looking till the ice gives way.

The seventh week. Blackborrow's foot has gone
gangrenous; McIlroy and Macklin need
to amputate the toes to save him. Wild
boils the instruments. Hurley stokes the fire
with penguin skins to get the chloroform
to vaporize. Blackborrow sinks away
under the fetid cloth; McIlroy peels
back the blackened flesh, takes the tin snips
Wild hands him, and the toes *plink* one by one
into a pail. When Blackborrow blinks awake
he wants a cigarette, so they roll one
with a page of *Britannica* — whittled
now to five volumes. That and the Boss's
everlasting Browning, a Walter Scott,
and a penny cookbook are what they call
the library. They read and reread, smoke
and sew and argue, pushing time behind
them like burrowing moles. Nightly Marston
gives dramatic readings from the cookbook,
ravishing them with pudding recipes
delectable with flour, till they sleep.

Water rustles over itself. The bay
shifts under silk. Wild wakes them, singing out
"Lash up and stow! The Boss may come today."

This is the morning ritual, performed
every day the weather's not so foul that
rescue lies beyond credence. They had thought
they could not bear a winter here. They are
bearing it. Seventeen hours of darkness
dusk to dawn, and the wind a lunatic.
It pries ice plates off the glacier and sails
them onto camp, a shower of windowpanes.

It drags Hussey down the beach to throw him
in the sea, so Hussey slams his pickax
in the shingle, self-arrests and hangs there
till the squall draws breath and he dare get up
and run for the hut. Bakewell considers
how wind wrings the air with anguish — low sobs,
moaning, cries of torment. He thinks it just
as well food is meager and occupies
their thoughts. "Otherwise our greatest peril
would be our minds." They hear a cracking boom
and rush out, knowing the sound of a ship's
signal guns, but it's the glacier rumbling.

The glacier calves. A huge wave lifts the bay,
it sprawls forward, someone shouts alarm — Ice
checks the torrent from sweeping them away.

Is there a world outside this world? Weather
is their only news. When the pack is out
and no wind, fog and dense silence close in
and fancies tug at them — that they must shout
to be heard, that they are turning to mist
themselves, that the island has come unmoored
and drifts to nowhere. They prefer the wind,
whose assault seems personal, the way it
wings rocks at their heads. The rocks are solid,
their heads are solid — it's reassuring.
Rarely, very rarely, a day comes still
and clear. The island lapses into grace.
"Sun settling in a mass of golden fire.
Many huge bergs, pale violet & pink,
sea deep indigo & snow peaks glowing."
Hurley climbs to a grotto and spares one
frame of film for its "magnificence of

icicles." For the rest he makes words do
for camera. All along it has been his
mind that could snick across a landscape, eyes
like shutters, freezing perfect specimens.
"The rocky scarps usually a greyblack,
still keep their natural color but appear
to shine with a gold veneer. A sunrise

of red clouds is reflected in the bay's
mirrory stillness. If we knew rescue
were coming, I could sit content and gaze."

One Hundred Days. No one says it aloud,
but few of them now believe that rescue
is coming. They still climb their lookout bluff
and scan the empty sea, a ritual for luck,
like touching wood, that no one thinks will work
but none dare omit. The Royal Thames Yacht
Club burgee flies from an oar pole, fraying
smaller as if measuring their hope. They've
slipped from hope to resignation, a soft
fall, really, like dropping into snow, thanks
to Wild. They all anchor to him; the stuff
Wild's made of doesn't fray. He keeps routine,
doles out chores, contrives holidays and treats —
on Saturdays tots served all round, "Gut Rot
1916" — methylated spirits
used formerly by Clark for preserving
specimens. That and a little sugar.
Down the hatch with the toast, "Sweethearts and wives."
The men are amused at how fond Wild is
of drinking it. He lets them use up hours
chaffering for last scraps of tobacco.
Wordie's got the most left and they appeal

to him as a geologist: a sailor
stands, pebble hidden behind his back — "I've
found the strangest stone, Jock. I'll give it you
for half a pipe-full of 'baccy." Wordie
has seen every rock on the spit six times
but he always relents. James, their scholar
and introvert, composes and presents
a ballad, with Hussey playing banjo:
My name is Frankie Wild-o and my hut's
on Elephant Isle. The wall's without a
single brick, the roof's without a tile-o.
Yet nevertheless you must confess by
many and many a mile, it's the most
palatial dwelling place you'll find on
Elephant Isle-o. Wild joins the chorus
with his rich bass voice. Thus they just manage

to avert their eyes from the blank bay
and the void that lies beyond. Wild keeps them
busy. Look to today. Only today.

They crouch dull-eyed and shaggy at the bay's
lip, prying up limpets, seaweed. They are
starving. *One hundred twenty-seven days.*

Wild

He is always calm, cool or collected, in open lanes
or in tight corners he is just the same.

The whalers at Grytviken have a saying for the extremity
of these latitudes. "Below 40 degrees is no Law. Beyond 50 is
no God." Here we sit at 61 degrees. Who knows what necessity

we've gone and gotten past the bounds of. I can't agree
with the whalers about God, I must say. In Antarctica
His face is passing strange but He still has eyes to see.

I tell the others it would be absurd to think that Providence
would give up on us now, having already put Itself to such
a deal of trouble for our sakes. Just look at the evidence

of all our close escapes. What was the good of those,
I tell them, if we're not meant to live? That God hears our prayers
has been already proved — if not always in the manner we suppose.

Nothing we suppose stands up to the truth of Polar Regions,
as I found out when I went the first time with Scott, and sailed
into the strangeness that is the Ice. Beyond 70 degrees is no Reason.

I've seen wind lift a man clean over my head; I've been tossed
myself off hands and knees and blown 20 yards before touching
ground again. I've had my hands so deeply bitten with frost

it looked as though I held a double handful of black plums.
I wonder if anyone can realize who hasn't had the experience,
what it means to own the pair of eyes that first plumbs

new country. The country seems to be making itself up
as you step into it. When the Boss and I were sledging toward the Pole
in thick drift, I had the weird sensation I was going to drop

any minute off the edge, as if the place ahead wasn't *there*
yet. Or you feel you are conjuring what you see by seeing it,
for the Ice is like something you might dream, by turns bizarre

and wondrous. When I with my Western Party sledged
along the coast, we came upon a bergschrund that was the wildest,
maddest and yet the grandest sight I've been privileged

to behold, a wide cavern of ice whose sheer ice walls were gashed
with caves of every blue. Glittering monuments and fairy palaces
rose around us from the cavern floor. We crossed ice bridges, lashed

to each other with alpine rope, such that only two men at a time
stood over the chasm. Looking into the crevasses you looked
into eternity. Just below its edge, a crevasse is a sublime

sky blue. From there it drops to utter black. "Hellholes,"
we called them. In the Antarctic, Hell looks like Heaven,
or else Heaven is as severe a place as Hell. The Poles

make you see everything in a different light, a light
like nowhere else. Standing in it rather spoils a person
for life in tamer places. Take this sunset tonight —

if it were blazing up behind the scrim of London, you'd think
it pretty enough. But here it is a sky to melt your eyes.
Ice has become my line of work; I can read water-sky and iceblink,

discern if floating ice is sea-ice or broken from a glacier
by whether it gives or shatters when struck. I know if a man
were made to face into a polar blizzard, he'd drown as sure

as if you held him underwater. You can't expel your breath
against such wind. And yet lying in your tent you're grateful
for it, as it will strip the surface of snow. If it's not the death

of you, it will make sledging easier. It strips men down
to bare facts, too. Some take the polish nicely
and shine up to something fine, while others are shown

to be grub-scoffing useless beggars. For real burnished
material, I say the Boss beats all, and I've been in the spot
to find out, when it was a race between frozen and famished,

and two men left behind us to die in their tent if we failed
to bring back rescue. Well, we rescued them, and the Boss
will rescue us. My own heart was very full when he sailed

that little boat away to get us help. I watched the black
speck of her from the lookout that afternoon, until she slipped
into the pack and out of my sight, and then I turned back

to my duty here. Which consists of settling squabbles,
contriving for the men what comfort I can and keeping them —
who range from sheer cussedness to loony in their foibles —

from turning murderous or suicidal. After dinner
and a sing-along I tuck up all the naughty children
and count another gladsome day. It will be a thinner

day tomorrow, I know well enough, for all Lees argues
that I don't. We gambled everything on the *Caird* —
a decent gamble with the Boss aboard, but if they lose

her, a few penguin steaks won't make a difference
to us one way or another. Not a soul but the men
on the *Caird* knows where we are, so our deliverance

rests with them. And when the Boss gets back I intend
turning all the party over to him in one piece. When we
were at Patience Camp and hungry, I learned to stand

at the floe's edge and flap my arms in imitation of a penguin
if we'd spotted a sea leopard, to lure it in. What's to be done
with such a skill as that, I wonder, in the wilds of London?

I dream, we all do, of hot baths, soft beds, tobacco
by the pipe-full, plates piled high with doughnuts — I'd like
mine cold with a little jam. And yet if I were back home

I'd soon be dreaming of the Ice. I know of nothing else
so ever-changing — if I explore forever I'll never see it all.
I've told the Boss: We're nothing but a couple of snow petrels.

IX. CROSSING TO STROMNESS
10—20 May 1916

Rise and not rest, but press
From earth's level where blindly creep
Things perfected, more or less,
To the heaven's height, far and steep

They stagger from the *Caird* and fling themselves
on their bellies, sucking water from a stream
that threads the rocky beach. They've landed with
their last strength on the iron coast.

                         Last night
wind drove them onshore till the cliffs became
the whole sky, black and murderous. They kept
their eyes down, bailing out the icy horror
that rose to freeze their hearts. Their teeth were clenched
against the next sound, the disemboweling
shriek of their keel ripped open on the rocks.
"What a pity," Worsley thought. "No one will
ever know we got so far." Then he dared
a glance up from the tiller. *She's clearing it!*
Some eddy or wind shift lent a sliver
of sea room, just as the gale sank away.
Combers struck the shoals and spouted upward,
"white beacon warnings" or watery ghosts
backlit by the darkness. But they'd slipped free.
Sudden the worst turns the best to the brave.
They stood offshore for one more night, and now

the beach sways under their unsteady legs.
The whaling stations — Grytviken, Husvik,
Stromness — all lie in harbors in the lee
of the island's mountains. Which is to say,
across the mountains from where the *Caird* lies
on the shingle. This side of the island
has no inhabitants but wreckage piled
at high-water mark — snapped masts, timbers, teak
stanchions capped with brass. The Boss finds
a child's toy ship — no less seaworthy than
their own boat is now with her planks chafed thin,
her caulking gone. By sea the stations are
beyond reach. One last task lies before them,
to go across by land, some thirty miles
of uncharted rock and ice, most of it
more vertical than not, as they can see
from where they stand. They haven't got the strength
to tote their sleeping bags or other gear
up those slopes. They'll have to make the crossing
in one rush, lightly equipped, march by day
and moonlight both, stopping only to eat.
It's to be the Boss, the Skipper, and Crean;
the others are played out. McNeish pulls screws
from the *Caird* ("A carpenter is a strange
bird; he can always go on producing
screws and nails"). He drives them through their boot soles
to give them purchase on the ice. They wait
a few days for clear weather, then set out
with the full moon hanging for a lantern.

When they're halfway up the first steep snowfield
a sea fog rises and envelops them.
Worsley is brought up short by some instinct

and finds there is a chasm at his feet.
The other two have vanished. Worsley's bones
turn liquid in his legs — then he hears Crean
almost at his elbow "cursing softly,"
and Shackleton saying, "Better rope up,
after this." They plod on, tied together.
The mist, the moonlight, and snow become one
substance; the men step into a glowing
nothingness and are jolted at each step
when the nothing goes solid underfoot.

They are in two worlds, each world a dream of
the other. In one world, six soaked bodies
tumble in breakers till they are cast up
on the shore and set upon by skuas.
Three determined ghosts rise from the bloody
flotsam and climb the island, their deaths
one next obstacle that will not stall them
from their purpose: to rescue their shipmates.
They are scraps of fog toiling through the fog.

In the other world three men snooze beneath
the *Caird* — capsized for a hut and snugly
turfed with tussock grass — while these others tramp
upland for all their sakes, invisible
but not bodiless. Each hauls his live breath
in and out and hears his heartbeat clubbing
in his ears. Snow creaks like a carriage wheel
under their feet. Night passes step by step,
men and sun mount slowly on blue ice, blue
sky. Above them, crags sift out of the mist.
Twice the three ascend to gaps between those black
fangs. Twice they face impossible descents

on the far side and turn back. Every climb
is grinding hours of effort, each repulse
a sinking of their hearts.

                 At the third pass
they straddle an ax-blade ridge and survey
what lies below — a sweep of ice and snow,
almost perpendicular. It's nearing dusk.
Fog rises again behind them, banners
of it streaming through the pass. The way back
"is blotted out, as though it had never
existed." There is no going but go
forward. Shackleton has McNeish's adze;
he hacks steps and the others follow — too
slow. If night overtakes them at this height
they'll freeze. Shackleton stops, considers, looks
at his companions. "We'll have to slide."
The slope below is lost in murky twilight.
It may be torn with rocks, it may empty
over a cliff; they can't tell. "Our chance is
a very small one indeed, but it is
up to us to take it." It has become
their creed: Dare to do what's laid before them
and trust Providence to turn the worst to
best. They coil the rope, sit toboggan-style
on the coils and push off.

                 Speed slams their hearts
shut, yanks their breath out by its roots and howls
a maelstrom past their ears. They are weightless,
plunging out of the world forever, time
unspooling wildly from its reel...

The world
catches hold, slows, eases to a halt in
a bank of snow. They get up, grope for breath,
pound snow off their shredded clothes and shake hands.
"It's not good to do that kind of thing too
often," is the Boss's comment. They start
across the snowfield, straining through the dark
to sense where crevasses wait to snatch them,
and then, mind-weary with the effort, stop
for a meal. While they eat, the jagged heights
above them start to radiate white auras,
brighter and brighter, and then the moon sails
into view. She trails a wake in the snow
that lights the way ahead.

Worsley remembers
when they were camped on the floes, how the walls
of the tents got threshed so thin that moonlight
drifted in on them and pipe-smoke drifted
out. All the fabric of the familiar —
that peopled, bustling life with its hallways,
pound notes, sparrows — it has all worn to gauze
in these three men, and things shadowy peer
through, shapely as the moon. "I again find
myself counting our party — Shackleton,
Crean, and I and — who is the other?" It
is a shared illusion. "It seems to me
that we are four, not three." They move across
a landscape of glass, in silence broken
by their own labors and deep-throated growls
of glaciers calving. The presence that stays
at the edge of sight, the unnameable fourth
of the party — whether it guides or stalks

or merely keeps company, whether it
is their hope, fear, or faith in Providence,
or their own patient deaths, they cannot say.

Twenty-seven hours ago they set out.
Day brings a high, feathered sky, a glaucous
sea below. They eat the last of the food.
By the chronometer slung round Worsley's
neck, it's seven in the morning and they
hear the Stromness steam whistle, calling men
to work. The old life lies within earshot.
They shake hands again and start down a pitch
"nearly perpendicular as a church
steeple," lying on their backs and kicking
steps with their heels. "A fine piece of level
country" reveals itself as a frozen
lake when Crean breaks through to his waist. They move
down a ravine, sloshing through the stream it
chivies downhill, and arrive at the wrong
end of a waterfall. They look at it,
one another, and the rope. They can see all
the pieces of what comes next but one — where
to tie the rope. Well. The Boss and Worsley
hold one end and toss the rest over; Crean
grabs it, slides away into the cascade,
and comes out spluttering below. That's one.
The Boss goes next with Worsley anchoring
the rope and Crean to break his fall. There's two.
Worsley frowns a look over the edge, stomps
his end of the rope onto the rocks, puts
his faith in friction and a swift rappel,
and lands doused but intact. He jerks the rope
to retrieve it and — the rope doesn't come.

They all three haul on it — nothing doing.
What can be holding the far end? They trade
glances, shrug, and turn away toward Stromness.

The rest is a stumbling walk on beach flats
malicious with ice. The whaling station's stench
comes out to meet them, flensed whales, whale offal.
The Primus stove is left behind with their
last meal, the rope still dangles in the falls.
They carry nothing now but McNeish's
adze, the logbook, exhaustion's dragging weight,
and the burden of rescue that they've borne
since Elephant Island fell behind them.

The first to see them at Stromness were two
boys, who ran off from them in fright. They looked
like ghosts or worse, men in rotting grave-clothes
with blackened skin. Was that cloth or flesh
that hung from them in tatters? And they reeked
like putrefaction. They walked on past sheds
where men looked and dodged away. Finally
a wary foreman led them to the door
of the station manager. A whaler
standing nearby heard the words that passed there.
"Manager he say: Who the hell are you?
and terrible bearded man in the centre
of the three say: My name is Shackleton."

X. ALL WELL?
21 May 1916–19 August 1939

Fancy that ridiculous Shackleton & his South Pole — in the crash
of the world. When all the sick & wounded have been tended…
then & not till then wd I concern myself with those penguins.

The Europe they knew had ceased to exist,
replaced by the equipage of nightmare.
Submarine warfare, aerial warfare,
entire nations in mortal agony
in the trenches. And twenty-two men,
last relics of that lost world, awaited
relief on Elephant Island, exposed
to the antique peril of starvation.

The Stromness whalers took Worsley to pluck
McNeish, Vincent, and McCarty from where
they were camped in the shelter of the *Caird*,
and they sailed at once for England and their
now divided fates. Shackleton borrowed
a British ship laid over in Husvik,
and sailed her, the *Southern Sky*, with Worsley,
Crean, and a Norwegian crew to rescue
his men with his own hands. "The third night out
the sea seemed to grow silent," admonished
by a film of ice. Seventy miles from
Elephant Island, pack ice turned them back.
It was the end of May. From Port Stanley
Shackleton cabled the Admiralty,

appealing for help. The Admiralty had
its hands full. It could send *Discovery* —
Scott's old ship — but not until October.

They can't hold out that long. Shackleton fumed,
drank, buttonholed every official he
could reach through half of South America.
Uruguay lent a trawler; they plowed south
again. Twenty miles from the island dense
fog and denser pack blocked them. Shackleton
paced the decks, aging with each thwarted hour.
Citizens of Punta Arenas next
raised funds to charter the *Emma*, an oak
schooner, but she wasn't built for the ice
that now lay like a cooper's iron band
around the island, and a gale drove them
back to Port Stanley. The governor there
suggested Sir Ernest possess himself
in patience till *Discovery* could arrive.
"The street of that port is about a mile
long, with the slaughter-house at one end and
the graveyard at the other. One may walk
from slaughter-house to graveyard, or for change
of scene stroll from graveyard to slaughter-house."
He could not summon that sort of patience.
July had come and gone. Chile offered
them the *Yelcho*, a dilapidated
lighthouse tender, a stubby steel affair
whose rusty hull would never stand the touch
of ice. A forlorn hope beat none at all,
so they sidled her down the latitudes.

One hundred twenty-eight days. The men sit
around the bogie stove, eyes keen on lunch

about to be served up, a watery
soup the optimists call stew. From outside
they hear Marston give a shout, then his feet
pounding down the shingle. "Hollerin' we
don't eat his portion," someone says, "while he's
out gazin' at the bergs." Marston lunges
through the canvas doorway. "Wild! There's a ship!
Oughtn't we light a flare?"

                              Bedlam. Men dive
out in all directions as if propelled
by an explosive charge. Wild lights a tin
of petrol, the others flail like maddened
windmills: *Here! Here we are! Here!* The *Yelcho*
lowers her lifeboat and as it closes
the shore, "Shackleton stands up in its bows,
crying out to Wild, 'Are you all well?' Wild
answers, 'All safe, Boss. All well.' "

                                 Three trips
and the boat pulls away a final time, then
puts about when Orde-Lees comes yelling
from the hut, where he's dawdled hoping
to show the Boss their handiwork. The Boss
is in no mood for guided tours. Lees jumps,
lands with a flop amidships and acquires
one concluding nickname: Always-Last.

Worsley recorded that the rescued men
walked about the ship's decks singing with joy.

The Great War promptly shoveled McCarty
and Cheetham under the waves. The Age of
Exploration had been eclipsed by something
far less personal, far more savage — though

Worsley, having sunk a U-boat, saved its
captain and cheerily shook hands. Holness,
whom the Boss yanked out of the sea that night
the floe split, signed on as a trawler-hand
and got swept overboard in a North Sea
storm, a man born to be drowned. They had each
been rescued into their single lives, where
rescue is snuffed out by the next event.

After the War, Shackleton sailed south once
more, on an ill-defined expedition
on an unlovely crank of a vessel
he named the *Quest*. With him went Wild, Worsley,
Macklin, McIlroy, Green, Kerr, Hussey, McLeod —
all singed by the Great Adventure and restless
to get near it again. Shackleton died
aboard the *Quest* at South Georgia, his always
balky heart stove in at forty-seven.

Wild went out to South Africa to try
cotton farming and foundered there on drought
and drink and lack of purpose. He lost his
farm, tended bar at four pounds a month, worked
on a railroad, worked in a quarry, kept
store for a Transvaal mine. Sometimes he sold
what he owned to pay the rent. When he died
his estate was this: his Polar medals.
A Johannesburg newspaper searched years
later for his grave. It could not be found.

In their journals the men spoke of Wild
the same way they spoke of the *Endurance*.
Our brave little ship. A great little man.
The Ice closed over *Endurance*; the Earth
over Frank Wild. What the Earth gets, the Earth keeps.

Crean. County Kerry

We went South meaning to explore the Ice. Instead the Ice
searched us — found what was in all our pockets, as you might say.
What was the worst of it, that time? Well, sir. One night watch
on the floes, I spotted a seal hauled up a hundred yards
from camp. We'd been on starvation rations, so right quick
I fetched Mr Wild, who came with his rifle and had it levelled when
what should that seal do but stand up on its back legs, no seal

at all but Jimmy James, retired behind a hummock to do life's duty.
Mr Wild and me, we looked at each other with full moons for eyes
and turned and went back to our tents without a word to anyone.
It adds to the cold, knowing your mistake near killed a man.
Finds the chinks in your nerve, it does. Plenty else was a misery
sure enough, but it was your own misery, if you take my meaning.
All you had to do was bear it, and no more than what the rest

was bearing along with you, the Boss included. Sir Ernest,
he was a splendid gentleman, and I done my duty towards him
to the end. Now here I am, back where I started life —
and with my own pub. There's some thinks the name I gave it
is meant as a brag on my adventures — *The South Pole.*
Ay, but I know the joke — *Here I stand at last!* There's a dream
I've had, all these years. I'm out alone on the Barrier again,

with Mr Evans like to die of scurvy in our tent, Lashly tending him
and me going for Hut Point to fetch help. The sun goes round
the way it did, stares in my eyes, looks in one ear, tries to see
through the back of my head. All about is white and white
and white and no sound but a tune I whistle for company.
Used to be, that dream was a nightmare and woke me in an icy sweat.
Now I wakes and laughs. *Well Tom,* says I. *So you haven't got there yet.*

South African Birds

What year?

The train chuffs from Cape Town to Johannesburg. A widow-bird flutters out
from the verge. White storks and cattle egrets conduct themselves about the
　　　　fields.

What year? Looking at the birds
will tell you where
you are, but they cannot tell you
when. Gravestones could name a year —
if you could find any gravestones.

Frank Hurley came home one afternoon from tramping with his camera
round the countryside and told his wife he felt unwell, but refused
to go to bed. He sat up in a chair, glaring straight before him
until he died next morning. And when Thomas Orde-Lees died,
didn't he get buried a few yards from McNeish, who had despised him.

Sometimes our deaths bear a remarkable resemblance to us,
causing sadness or relief as we did, possessed
of Hurley's dauntless eye or obtruding
in the irksome manner Orde-Lees was known for all his life.

Red-billed wood hoopoes up-
end themselves on their perches, tails
flung uppermost,
and give out cackling whoops of laughter.

And then our deaths grow old and perish.

The men whose lives Frank Wild helped to save are all
long dead. Their deaths have fallen
so far behind us they are become, as Worsley would say,
quaint.

While the other Kingdom
of the Warm-Blooded comes back
season after season
in all their feathers, immortality
with flesh on it,
or sometimes more metallurgy
than flesh.

A malachite sunbird displays from a branch.
Jade on fire.

What year?

If there were a heaven for us
it would be release from the hurtling-
forwardness, the locomotive of time. We would step down
among bronze-winged coursers, gray
louries, hadedas, blacksmith plovers with their lurching gait,
little bee-eaters.

Though not without grief. We would not be ourselves without
our plumage of sorrows. Only
that we would not fade.

Frank Wild keeps store outside a hellhole
Zulu mine, exhausted from years
of killing work. He leans on the counter
and leans

into the tiller of the *Caird*. Ahead
an island's glacier gleams
out of the dark. Silver petrels
shimmer past him,
shards
of the ice-light of which he is a part,
calm as the wild moon.

Notes

Quotations from the men's journals are indicated with the writer's last name and date of entry. These and other quotations and points of fact are from the following sources, abbreviated in the notes as shown:

Alexander   Alexander, Caroline. *The Endurance: Shackleton's Legendary Antarctic Expedition.* Alfred A. Knopf. New York. 1998.

ATL   From papers held by the Alexander Turnbull Library. Wellington, New Zealand.

Bakewell   From the unpublished autobiography of William Bakewell, in the possession of his daughter, Mrs. Elizabeth Rajala.

Cherry-Garrard   Cherry-Garrard, Apsley. *The Worst Journey in the World.* Carroll & Graf Publishers, Inc. New York. 1989. (First published in Great Britain in 1922.)

Fisher   Fisher, Margery and James. *Shackleton.* James Barrie Books, Ltd. London. 1957.

Greenstreet   From Lionel Greenstreet's journal and letters, all in possession of the Greenstreet family.

Heacox   Heacox, Kim. *Shackleton: The Antarctic Challenge.* National Geographic. Washington, D.C. 1999.

Huntford   Huntford, Roland. *Shackleton.* Fawcett Columbine. New York. 1985.

Lansing   Lansing, Alfred. *Endurance: Shackleton's Incredible Voyage.* Carroll & Graf Publishers, Inc. New York. 1986. (First published in New York in 1959.)

Macklin   From Alexander Macklin's journal and an unpublished narrative ("Shackleton As I Knew Him"), both in the possession of the Macklin family.

Mills   Mills, Leif. *Frank Wild.* Caedmon of Whitby. Whitby, North Yorkshire. 1999.

ML	From papers held by the Mitchell Library, State Library of New South Wales. Sydney, Australia.
RGSSA	From papers held by the Royal Geographical Society of South Australia.
Shackleton (annot)	Shackleton, Ernest. *South: The Story of Shackleton's Last Expedition, 1914–1917.* Edited and annotated by Peter King. Trafalgar Square Publishing. North Pomfret, Vermont. 1991.
Shackleton, South	Shackleton, Ernest. *South: A Memoir of the Endurance Voyage.* Carroll & Graf Publishers, Inc. New York. 1998. (First published in Great Britain in 1919.)
SPRI	From papers held by the Scott Polar Research Institute. University of Cambridge.
Thomson	Thomson, John. *Shackleton's Captain: A Biography of Frank Worsley.* Mosaic Press. Toronto. 1999.
Wild (Memoirs)	Wild, Frank. "Memoirs." Unpublished manuscript held by the Mitchell Library, State Library of New South Wales. Sydney, Australia. Probably written about 1937.
Wild, Quest	Wild, Frank. *Shackleton's Last Voyage: The Story of the Quest.* Frederick A. Stokes Company. New York. 1924.
Worsley, Boat Journey	Worsley, F. A. *Shackleton's Boat Journey.* W. W. Norton & Company. New York and London. 1977. (First published in Great Britain in 1933.)
Worsley, Endurance	Worsley, F. A. *Endurance.* W. W. Norton & Company. New York and London. 1999. (First published in Great Britain in 1931.)

"Immense clouds of dark vapour rolled skyward from the water, as if from a
boiling lake. These mists solidified into crystals, which fell in shimmering
showers from the clear blue sky — a rain of jewels. The sun shone through
the glinting fall in great rainbow circles, which spanned the sky. The crystal
showers carpeted the pack ice and ship until she looked like a tinselled
beauty on a field of diamonds." Hurley. March 1915? *ML*. Quoted in
Heacox.

"[They] rushed along as fast as their legs could carry them yelling out 'Clark!
Clark!'" Worsley. 8 January 1915. *ATL*. Quoted in *Huntford.*

"I really think that for scenery I have never seen anything to equal that in
amongst which we find ourselves today." Orde-Lees. *ATL*. Quoted in
Alexander.

"Rope pulling makes the hands sore & the ropes are exceedingly dirty & tarry
but it is good exercise." Orde-Lees. *ATL*. Quoted in *Alexander.*

"All hands were engaged during the day in rubbing shoots off our potatoes."
Shackleton, South.

"There was a clatter aft during the afternoon, and Hussey, who was at the wheel,
explained that: 'The wheel spun round and threw me over the top of it.'"
Shackleton, South.

Shackleton

"Never for me the lowered banner, / never the last endeavour." From a letter
written by Shackleton to Mrs. John Rowett. 18 July 1921. *SPRI*. Quoted in
Alexander.

Ernest Shackleton went out to Antarctica four times, first with Scott on the
1901–1904 expedition (he was invalided home before the second winter),
then three expeditions of his own: an attempt to be the first to the Pole in
1907–1909, on the *Endurance*, and finally on the *Quest*.

"A live donkey is better than a dead lion, isn't it?" Shackleton, quoted in a letter written by his wife, Emily Shackleton, to H. R. Mill. 16 August 1922. *SPRI*. Quoted in *Huntford*.

"One who never turned his back but marched breast forward, / Never doubted clouds would break, / Never dreamed, though right were worsted, wrong would triumph, / Held we fall to rise, are baffled to fight better, / Sleep to wake." Robert Browning, "Epilogue" (to *Asolando*). Shackleton's favorite poet.

"I am just good as an explorer, and nothing else." Shackleton in a letter to his wife. 26 October 1914. *SPRI*. Quoted in *Huntford*.

"The old trick! Only I discern — / Infinite passion, and the pain / Of finite hearts that yearn." Robert Browning, "Two in the Campagna."

"What the ice gets, the ice keeps." Shackleton. Quoted in *Worsley, Endurance*.

Pressure

"We must possess ourselves in patience till a Southerly gale occurs or the ice opens of its own sweet will." Worsley. 24 January 1915. *ATL*. Quoted in *Heacox*.

"Spreading out till they meet, forming long and beautiful snow-cliffs, washed at their bases by the waters of illusion." *Worsley, Endurance*, quoting his trip log.

"Wild was such a tremendously approachable fellow, and always so outstandingly ready to help in every possible way." Macklin, from an interview with James Fisher. *SPRI*. Quoted in *Huntford*.

"Wild was a wonderful foil to Shackleton…with his Irish temperament." Greenstreet, from an interview with James Fisher. *SPRI*. Quoted in *Huntford*.

"I say, Doctor, don't you think we are better off than the King…." Cheetham. Quoted in *Macklin*. Also quoted in *Huntford*.

"No one knows what it means to me to have a bicycle and a place to ride it, however rough & heavy the going." Orde-Lees. 11 March 1915. *ATL*. Quoted in *Huntford*.

"Hurley is a warrior with his camera & would go anywhere or do anything to get a picture." From a letter written by Greenstreet to his father. 17 November 1914. Quoted in *Huntford*.

"With cheerful Australian profanity he...snaps his snap or winds his handle turning out curses of delight & pictures of life by the fathom." Worsley. 24 January 1915. *ATL*. Quoted in *Huntford*.

"Took color camera to lead this morning amidst similar gorgeous conditions of yesterday & more glorified perhaps for a fine crop of ice flowers springing up on the lead & they, illuminated by the morning sun, resembled a field of pink carnations." Hurley. *ML*. Quoted in *Alexander*.

"An enormous train with squeaky axles... Mingled with this were the sound of steamer whistles starting to blow...& underfoot moans & groans of damned souls in torment." Worsley. 10 June 1915. *ATL*. Quoted in *Huntford*.

"A terrible noise, as of a thousand guns going off...The *Endurance* was lying on her side — squeezed up and out of the ice and flung over."
Worsley, Endurance.

"The ship can't live in this, Skipper.... What the ice gets, the ice keeps."
Shackleton. Quoted in *Worsley, Endurance*.

"We do not see why men should have all the glory, & women none, especially when there are women just as brave & capable as there are men." Letter sent to Shackleton. 11 January 1914. *Fisher*.

"Last night we drank the health of our Sweethearts & Wifes." McNeish, 23 October 1915. *ATL*. Quoted in *Huntford*. "Some wag invariably adding 'and may they never meet.'" Hussey. Quoted in *Mills*.

Crean. Night Watch

Once the *Endurance* was beset, the night watch became a time when the men often sat up around the stove, telling stories.

"Many were solicitous...that my behaviour on reaching civilization should be above reproach. As for Crean, they said things that ought to have made him blush; but what would make Crean blush would make a butcher's dog drop its bone." *Worsley, Boat Journey.*

Tom Crean made three trips to Antarctica: with Scott in 1901–1904 and 1910–1912, and with Shackleton on the *Endurance.* Crean was with the search party that found Scott and his companions dead in their tent.

Oamaru (pronounced *Ah-mah-roo´*): a port on the South Island of New Zealand.

"With untiring persistence the little lighthouse blinked out the message, 'What ship's that? What ship's that?' They were obviously puzzled and disturbed at getting no answer." *Cherry-Garrard.*

Apsley Cherry-Garrard wrote that when Scott told Crean he was to be with the party that was turning back to base camp, rather than make the final dash to the South Pole, Crean was in tears. *Cherry-Garrard.*

"We saw the party ahead in inverted mirage some distance above their heads." "Birdie" Bowers (Crean's sledge mate). Quoted in *Cherry-Garrard.*

"There are many questions which ought to be studied…. Whence came…X's blue eyes: for he started from England with brown ones and his mother refused to own him when he came back?" *Cherry-Garrard.*

What the Ice Gets

"Out of whose womb came the ice…." From the Book of Job; verse torn by Shackleton from a Bible he left on the ice (but which McLeod retrieved) after the *Endurance* was crushed.

"Every muscle ached and revolted at the unspeakable toil…. Every spell was an agony." Macklin. 28 October 1915. *Macklin.*

"At the beginning the ship's sides had buckled in and out as though she had been a concertina…. It gave me the horrible impression that the ship was gasping for breath." *Worsley, Endurance.*

"Do you hear that, we'll none of us get home again." Macklin. 28 October 1915. *Macklin.*

"You could hear the ship being crushed up, the ice being ground into her, and you almost felt your own ribs were being crushed. It seemed the end of everything." Greenstreet. *Greenstreet.* Quoted in *Shackleton (annot).*

"Nobody had the common decency to say thank you. And Frank Wild's remark was, 'Would any gentleman like his boots cleaned.'" Walter How, from an interview with James Fisher. *SPRI*. Quoted in *Huntford*. Worsley's version (in *Worsley, Endurance*): "If any of you gentlemen would like your boots blacked, would you kindly leave them outside the hotel door?"

"A terrible night, with the ship sullen dark against the sky & the noise of the pressure against her...seeming like the cries of a living creature." Reginald James's journal. 27 October 1915. *SPRI*. Quoted in *Huntford*.

"Ship and stores have gone — so now we'll go home." *Macklin*. Quoted in *Huntford*.

McNeish & Hurley

"A man must shape himself to a new mark directly the old one goes to ground." Shackleton. *Shackleton, South*.

"I am afraid it is all up with the ship." McNeish. 24 October 1915. *ATL*. Quoted in *Huntford*.

"The ice has cut clean through the ship." McNeish. 28 October 1915. *ATL*.

"I have placed my Loved ones fotos inside my Bible we got presented with from Queen Alexandra & put them in my bag." McNeish. 1 August 1915. *ATL*. Quoted in *Huntford*.

"The clock is ticking on the wall as we take a final leaving of the cosy wardroom." Hurley. 27 October 1915. *ML*. Quoted in *Huntford*.

In his journal entry on 27 October, Hurley called the forces destroying the ship "the ice mill." *ML*. Quoted in *Huntford*.

While the expedition was beset in the ice of the Weddell Sea, the only prominent "landmarks" in the vicinity were icebergs, whose positions relative to the ship were noted as a sign of the currents that moved the ice and the ship with it. The largest bergs were given names; one of the most distinctive of these was dubbed "Rampart Berg." *Shackleton, South*.

"I have only a saw hammer & chisel & adze but we are managing all right." McNeish. 18 November 1915. *ATL*. Quoted in *Huntford*.

"The chipping of two holes fifteen inches in diameter with a blunt flat chisel [was] a somewhat arduous undertaking." Hurley. 5 November 1915. *ML*. Quoted in *Huntford*.

"I dont see how we could have better luck than we had had. We have never had a religious service since the second out from Plymouth." McNeish. 18 July 1915. *ATL*. Quoted in *Huntford*.

Ocean Camp

"Yes, but we are not going to let the ice get us." Frank Wild, after Shackleton had told Worsley the ship was doomed, as reported in *Worsley, Endurance*.

"It is just like school-days over again, and very jolly it is, too, for the time being!" One of the men's journals, quoted in *Shackleton, South*.

"Without her our destitution seems more emphasized, our desolation more complete." From one of the men's journals, reported in *Shackleton, South*.

"We were now very lonely." *Bakewell*. Quoted in *Alexander*.

"The Crew agree to conduct themselves in an orderly, faithful, honest and sober manner and…to be obedient to the lawful commands of the said Master, or of any Person who shall lawfully succeed him…whether on board, in boats or on shore." Ship's Articles, from the BOT Crew List. Quoted in *Huntford*.

Waiting Waiting Waiting

"Waiting. / Waiting. / Waiting." Entry in Shackleton's journal. 26 January 1916. *SPRI*. Quoted in *Huntford*.

"All around us we have day after day the same unbroken whiteness unrelieved by anything at all." Macklin. 13 March 1916. *Macklin*. Quoted in *Lansing*.

"Nothing to do, nowhere to walk, no change in surroundings, food or anything. God send us open water soon or we shall go balmy." Greenstreet. January 1915. *SPRI*. Quoted in *Lansing*.

"A bug on a single molecule of oxygen in a gale of wind would have about the same chance of predicting where he was likely to finish up." James. 11 February 1916. *SPRI*. Quoted in *Lansing*.

"Nothing to do, see or say." James. March 1916. *SPRI*. Quoted in *Lansing*.

"The worst thing is having to kill time. It seems such a waste." James. February 1916. *SPRI*. Quoted in *Lansing*.

"In all directions we hear Adélie making quaint noises — like men talking in deep tones...." Worsley. 10 March 1916. *ATL*. Quoted in *Huntford*.

"Stewed penguin heart, liver, eyes, tongues, toes & God knows what else, with a cup of water." McNeish. February 1916. *ATL*. Quoted in *Lansing*.

"This duty fell upon me & was the worst job I ever had in my life."
Wild (Memoirs). ML.

"I remember taking him out when he was a puppy in my pocket, only his nose peeping out and getting covered with frost." Macklin. January 1916. *Macklin*. Quoted in *Lansing*.

"I've just brought a bit of Nelson for you to try." Crean. Quoted in *Lansing*.

"One man put copper wire round his belly; thought he was going to walk home." Green. Interview with James Fisher. *SPRI*. Quoted in *Huntford*.

"His 6 tunes is heartbreaking." McNeish. 8 February 1916. *ATL*. Quoted in *Huntford*.

"The *Daily Mail* had the heading about us, 'Compulsory Trans Antarctic Expedition.'" Worsley. 29 January 1916. *ATL*. Quoted in *Huntford*.

"[Tried] to drown multicoloured hounds.... My endeavours were not fraught with great success, for...after assuming the form of seals, [they] eyed me complacently with gummy eyes." Hurley. 6 March 1916. *ML*. Quoted in *Huntford*.

"I long for some rest, free from thought." Shackleton. January 1916. *SPRI*. Quoted in *Lansing*.

"I long for a place where the direction of the wind does not matter a Tinker's cuss." James. 8 February 1916. *SPRI*. Quoted in *Lansing*.

"The skipper says he has seen it, but we know him to be a liar." McNeish. 26 February 1916. *ATL*. Quoted in *Lansing*.

"Pray God we may find a landing here." Macklin. April 1916. *Macklin*. Quoted in *Lansing*.

"Cheered all up the sight of land. Please God we will soon get ashore." Shackleton. 23 March 1916. The last entry in his journal. *SPRI*. Quoted in *Huntford*.

Orde-Lees

"Well Old Lady. We've got it in the neck all right this time, haven't we?"
  Shackleton's remark to Orde-Lees as they abandoned the *Endurance*.
  Orde-Lees' response: "Well, no, I don't think so. You wouldn't have had
  anything to write a book about, if it hadn't been for this." Orde-Lees.
  "Beset by Berg and Floe." *SPRI.* Quoted in *Huntford.*
"[I have] always been susceptible to sea-sickness [and] was immediately
  convinced that the only cause…must be…heaving of our floe during the
  night." Orde-Lees. "Beset by Berg and Floe." *SPRI.* Quoted in *Huntford.*

Open Water

"I never saw, / Nor shall see, here or elsewhere, till I die, / Not tho' I live three
  lives of mortal men, / So great a miracle…." Lines from Tennyson's "Morte
  d'Arthur," which Macklin said kept running through his head. *Lansing.*
"Ghostly shadows of silver, snow and fulmar petrels flashed close to us."
  Shackleton, South.
"Occasionally from an almost clear sky came snow-showers, falling silently on
  the sea and laying a thin shroud of white over our bodies and our boats."
  Shackleton, South.
"We thought we saw a great berg bearing down upon us, its form outlined
  against the sky, but this startling spectacle resolved itself into a low-lying
  cloud in front of the rising moon." *Shackleton, South.*
"Twankedillo, twankedillo, and my roaring pair of bagpipes made from the
  green willow." Marston's song as described by Macklin. 14 April 1916.
  Macklin. Quoted in *Huntford.*
"Always the same confident, blue-eyed little man, unmoved by cold or fatigue."
  Shackleton. Quoted in *Worsley, Boat Journey.*
"Wild sat at the rudder with the same calm, confident expression that he would
  have worn under happier conditions; his steel-blue eyes looked out to the
  day ahead." *Shackleton, South.*
"It was a stern night." *Shackleton, South.*

"The night of the 14th was the worst I have ever known." *Wild (Memoirs)*. *ML*.

"Think we are getting out to sea & lost." Orde-Lees. 14 April 1916. *ATL*. Quoted in *Huntford*.

"Dawn at last & find ourselves bang in front of land." Orde-Lees. 15 April 1916. *ATL*. Quoted in *Huntford*.

"It was the extreme Eastern end of the island which we had just managed to grasp as the storm drove us past." James. 15 April 1916. *SPRI*. Quoted in *Huntford*.

"Little Frankie Wild...alone of all the party looked something like his normal self." Macklin. *Macklin*. Quoted in *Huntford*.

"How delicious to wake in one's sleep & listen to the chanting of the penguins mingling with the music of the sea." Hurley. April 1916. *ML*. Quoted in *Lansing*.

Worsley

"A rather wild, excitable, hare-brained, half grown up, kind of customer quite incapable of responsible action." Macklin describing the men's view of Worsley before he proved his genius in the boats. *Macklin*. Quoted in *Huntford*.

"The turmoil of sound made it seem as though ghostly trains were rushing past the ship — trains of snow." *Worsley, Endurance*.

"It's not much like the Riviera." *Worsley, Endurance*.

"Wuzzles" was a play on the name Worsley — a rather cheeky nickname for the captain of a ship, but Worsley's shipmates bestowed it on him in response to his loopy behavior. Later, when Worsley proved his remarkable worth in the boats, "Wuzzles" became a term of affection from the men.

"Ran out on the floe in a state of nature & had a brief — a very brief — snow bath.... Poor Crean...catching sight of me naked in the snow nearly fainted — thinking I'd 'gone wrong in the napper.'" Worsley. 17 April 1915. *ATL*. Quoted in *Huntford*.

"We experienced colour in a way unknown outside the far North or South. It was as though our snowy surroundings were being painted upon continually by a master-hand." *Worsley, Endurance*.

Worsley took a "longitude of Mercury 'for swank'...'not many people can boast
of having done so.'" Worsley. 21 September 1915. *ATL*. Quoted in *Huntford*.

"*Endurance* crushed and abandoned in 69°5' S. and 51°35' W. All hands
to-morrow proceeding to the westward. All well. December 23rd, 1915.
E. H. Shackleton." *Worsley, Endurance.*

"It seemed as though we had come upon some marvellous city of ice.... The
illusion was so perfect...many of us would not have been surprised had we
been hailed by voices." *Worsley, Endurance.*

"There was something unspeakably grim in the sight of grown men playing on a
beach rather like children on the sands at an English seaside town." *Worsley,
Endurance.*

"I swore we would 'Get to wind'ard or sink the bitch.'" *Worsley, Boat Journey.*

"I remember the guffaw that went up when one of the company remarked, 'The
boat's sure to be safe if the Skipper's in it. He wasn't born to be
drowned'.... it took some time before I realised the inference that I was
born to be hanged!" *Worsley, Endurance.*

The James Caird

"Superhuman effort isn't worth a damn unless it achieves results." Shackleton.
Quoted in *Worsley, Endurance.*

"Some of the party...had become despondent, & were in a 'What's the use' sort
of mood & had to be driven to work, none too gently either."
Wild, (Memoirs). ML.

"Skinning them...was painful work, for to bare the hand...in such a blizzard
means almost certain frostbite.... it was only the warmth of the dead
penguins that saved our hands." Orde-Lees. 19 April 1916. *ATL*. Quoted in
Lansing.

"I was haunted by a series of pictures...of what would become of these men
should our attempt fail.... I felt as though I could not get my fill of gazing at
them." *Worsley, Endurance.*

"I have every confidence in you and always have had, May God prosper your
work and your life. You can convey my love to my people and say I tried my

best." From letter left by Shackleton with Wild on Elephant Island. Quoted in *Lansing*.

"With a final wave of the hand, and three squawky cheers from us and the penguins, Sir Ernest and his crew set off on their perilous journey." Orde-Lees. 24 April 1916. *ATL*. Quoted in *Huntford*.

"Castles, towers, and churches swayed unsteadily around us.... Swans of weird shape pecked at our planks, a gondola steered by a giraffe ran foul of us, which much amused a duck sitting on a crocodile's head." *Worsley, Boat Journey*.

"We got the reefed jib off the main...set reefed lug and mizzen, and with these large handkerchiefs endeavoured to claw offshore." *Worsley, Boat Journey*.

"Old Jamaica": sailors' slang, a name for the sun.

"Go to sleep Crean & don't be clucking like an old hen." From Worsley's navigation book kept during the boat journey. *SPRI*. Quoted in *Alexander*.

"Even when cracked lips...checked the outward and visible signs of amuse-ment... We laughed, or rather gurgled with laughter." *Shackleton, South*.

"There was a small bird, unknown to me, that appeared always to be in a fussy, bustling state.... It irritated me. It had practically no tail, and it flitted about vaguely as though in search of the lost member." *Shackleton, South*.

"Most unfabl. [unfavourable] conditions of Obs....the boat was jumping like a flea." Worsley's navigation log. 7 May 1916. *SPRI*. Quoted in *Huntford*.

"The sight of these birds is a guarantee that you are within fifteen miles of land." *Worsley, Boat Journey*.

" 'Sea room, sea room, or a change of wind' was our mental prayer.... six men driving a boat slamming at the seas and steadily bailing death overboard." *Worsley, Boat Journey*.

"The gale and sea were too much for us." *Worsley, Endurance*.

"The night wore on. We were very tired. We longed for day." *Shackleton, South*.

"Only three or four of the giant deep-sea swells separated us from the cliffs of destruction — the coast of death." *Worsley, Boat Journey*.

"Miss Sir E. very much…. We expect relief in about a fortnight." Hurley. 27
  April 1916. *ATL*. Quoted in *Huntford*.

"Great confidence is reposed in crew…. The Caird is an excellent sailer….How
  we shall count the days." Hurley. 24 April 1916. *ATL*. Quoted in *Huntford*.

"I heard one of the few pessimists remark, 'That's the last of them' & almost
  knocked him down with a rock, but satisfied myself by addressing a few
  remarks to him in real lower deck language." *Wild (Memoirs). ML.*

"Then seeing some of the party in tears I immediately set them all to work."
  Wild (Memoirs). ML.

"A horrible pessimist…. I had to threaten to shoot him to make him keep his
  tongue between his teeth." Wild. Letter to Ellen Augusta James.
  31 December 1916. *RGSSA*. Quoted in *Huntford*.

"Roll up your bags, boys. The 'Boss' may be coming back to-day." Wild. Quoted
  in *Worsley, Endurance*. "Wild rouses all hands with a lusty 'Lash up and
  stow!'" James. 18 May 1916. *SPRI*. Quoted in *Huntford*.

"Had we had plenty to eat and to smoke, our minds would have been on our real
  peril." *Bakewell*. Quoted in *Alexander*.

"Magnificent golden sunset, sun…settling in a mass of golden fire…. Many huge
  bergs appear pale violet & pink, sea a deep indigo & snow peaks behind first
  golden then aglow with alpengluh." Orde-Lees. *ATL*. Quoted in *Huntford*.

"Go walking with Wild. We visit a neighboring cavern in the glacier which was
  adorned with a magnificence of icicles." Hurley. 5 July 1916. *ML*. Quoted in
  Alexander.

"A sunrise of bright red clouds reflected in the mirrory stillness of the bay….
  The rocky scarps ordinarily a greyblack, still kept their natural color but
  appeared to shine with a golden veneer." Hurley. *ML*. Quoted in *Alexander*.

"This one would not tire of provided we knew Sir E. & the crew of the 'Caird'
  were safe & when relief could be definitely expected." Hurley. 16 July 1916.
  ML. Quoted in *Huntford*.

"My name is Frankie Wild-o…." As quoted by A. G. E. Jones, "Frankie Wild's
  Hut," *Journal of the Royal Naval Medical Service*, Vol. 64, Spring 1978, p. 54.
  Quoted in *Huntford*.

Wild "was always calm, cool or collected, in open lanes or in tight corners he
was just the same; but when he did tell a man to jump that man jumped
pretty quick." Macklin. *Macklin.* Quoted in *Huntford.*

"'Below 40 degrees is no law,' the whalers would say, 'beyond 50 degrees is no
God.'" *Heacox.*

"The same God who has kept us so far will be watching over us and that He
hears your prayers has been already proved." Wild in a letter written to Miss
Anderson while on Scott's first expedition. 26 February 1903. *ATL.* Quoted
in *Mills.*

Frank Wild made five trips to Antarctica, with Scott (1901–1904), with
Shackleton in his attempt to be first to the Pole (1907–1909), with Sir
Douglas Mawson (1911–1912), and on Shackleton's last two expeditions, on
the *Endurance* and the *Quest.*

"Once Harrison was blown clean over my head, lifted quite twenty feet." Wild's
journal from the Mawson Expedition. 5 September 1912. *Mills.*

"I have been picked up off my hands & knees & thrown more than twenty yards
without touching anything." *Wild (Memoirs). ML.*

"My fingers had blistered very badly and looked as though I were holding a
double handful of black plums." *Wild (Memoirs). ML.*

"It was like walking into a white blanket, & I had a weird feeling that any minute
I should come to the edge and fall off." Wild, describing his 1908 sledging
journey with Shackleton. *Wild (Memoirs). ML.*

"An enormous cavern over a thousand feet wide & four hundred feet deep
with crevasses at the bottom which appear to have no bottom. The sides
splintered & gashed with caves of every blue from the palest blue to black &
the whole thing glittering in the sun.... The whole was the wildest maddest
& yet the grandest thing imaginable." *Wild (Memoirs). ML.*

"Waves & hills, monuments, statues & fairy palaces in all directions, from a few
feet to over three hundred feet in height." *Wild (Memoirs). ML.*

"I lengthened the harness with alpine rope to allow more scope and prevent
more than two being in a crevasse at the same time." Wild's journal of his
sledging journey on Mawson's expedition. 15 March 1912. *Mills.*

"If a man was made to face a wind of 100 miles an hour, he would be dead as quickly as though held under water, the force being so great that he would not be able to expel his breath." *Wild (Memoirs). ML.*

"If we had only had Joyce and Marston here instead of these two grub scoffing useless beggars we would have done it easily." Wild's journal of his attempt with Shackleton and two others (the "useless beggars") to reach the South Pole. 31 December 1908. *SPRI.* Quoted in *Mills.*

"and two men left behind us...." On the return journey of Shackleton's attempt to reach the Pole in 1909, when the party was still some miles from base camp, one of the men became too ill to continue. He was left in the care of another man while Shackleton and Wild hiked twenty-seven hours with few stops and no sleep to fetch help.

"My own heart was very full.... At 4 p.m. I climbed the rocks & through the binoculars caught a last glimpse of the boat just as she disappeared amongst the pack ice." *Wild (Memoirs). ML.*

"Almost every night...disputes would arise...& I had to go along & tell one or other to move over, & could not turn in myself until all the naughty children were nicely tucked up." *Wild (Memoirs). ML.*

"When open leads occurred near Patience Camp sea leopards were sometimes seen swimming about & I got three on different occasions by pretending to be a penguin. I stooped down near the water waving my arms up & down like flippers, & the sea leopard came charging at a terrific rate through the water & shot out onto the ice." *Wild (Memoirs). ML.*

"I like them [doughnuts] cold with a little jam." Wild. Quoted by Hurley in *Lansing.*

"I know of nothing else that can assume such fantastic shapes & take such marvellous variety of colour." *Wild (Memoirs). ML.*

Crossing to Stromness

"Rise and not rest...." Robert Browning, "Reverie."

"The thoughts of the others I did not know — mine were regret for having brought my diary and annoyance that no one would ever know we had got so far." *Worsley, Boat Journey.*

"Rollers...topped up on the shoals, spouted white beacon warnings on the reefs, and hurled their loud shouting cohorts on the black spears of the rocky headlands." *Worsley, Boat Journey.*

"For sudden the worst turns the best to the brave." Robert Browning, "Prospice." Shackleton quoted and paraphrased this line several times in his description of the crossing in *South*.

"There were ships' masts and timbers, a great mainyard, bits of figureheads, teak stanchions with brass caps." *Worsley, Endurance.*

"A carpenter is a strange bird — prolific as a *Daily Mail* Wyandotte. He can always go on producing screws and nails — speak to him kindly and he'll lay another in your hand." *Worsley, Boat Journey.*

"The relief of hearing Shackleton's voice, and then that of Crean, who was cursing softly, was indescribable.... 'Better rope up, after this,' said Shackleton." *Worsley, Endurance.*

"A heavy sea-fog had come up and blotted out the country we had traversed as completely as though it had never existed." *Worsley, Endurance.*

"Our chance was a very small one indeed, but it was up to us to take it." *Worsley, Endurance.*

"It's not good to do that kind of thing too often." Shackleton. Quoted in *Worsley, Endurance.*

"While writing this seven years after (almost), each step of that journey comes back clearly, and even now I again find myself counting our party — Shackleton, Crean, and I and — who was the other?" *Worsley, Boat Journey.*

"I know that during that long and racking march of thirty-six hours over the unnamed mountains and glaciers of South Georgia it seemed to me often that we were four, not three." *Shackleton, South.*

"Nearly as perpendicular as a church steeple." *Worsley, Endurance.*

"Our spirits rose when we found ourselves on a fine piece of level country." *Worsley, Endurance.*

"It was the splashing of a waterfall, and we were at the wrong end." *Shackleton, South.*

"Manager say: 'Who the hell are you?' and terrible bearded man in the centre of the three say very quietly: 'My name is Shackleton.' Me — I turn away and weep." A Mr. Mansell, quoted in *Shackleton (annot).*

"Fancy that ridiculous Shackleton...." Winston Churchill in a letter to his wife, from Flanders. 28 March 1916. Quoted in *Huntford*.

"On the third night out the sea seemed to grow silent." *Shackleton, South.*

"The street of that port is about a mile and a half long. It has the slaughter-house at one end and the graveyard at the other. The chief distraction is to walk from the slaughter-house to the graveyard. For a change one may walk from the graveyard to the slaughter-house." *Shackleton, South.*

"Hollerin' we don't eat his portion..." This is the author's rendering of a story told in several accounts of the rescue (including Worsley in his *Endurance*). The men in the hut thought Marston was shouting because he was late for lunch and feared the others would leave no portion of the scant meal for him.

"When the boat was within calling reach, Shackleton stood up in its bows, crying out to Wild, 'Are you all well?' To which Wild answered, 'All safe, Boss, all well.'" Hussey, in an interview with the BBC, quoted in *Walking Out of History: The True Story of Shackleton's Endurance Expedition.* American Radio Works. Minnesota Public Radio. 1999.

"The men, still very excited, were wandering round the ship, talking, laughing, even singing." *Worsley, Endurance.*

Frank Wild died in South Africa on 19 August 1939.

"Many years later — in 1966 — the Johannesburg daily newspaper, *The Star*, reported a search for Wild's grave. It could not be found." *Mills.*

"[Our] brave little ship." *Worsley, Endurance.*

"Frank Wild was a great little man." Eric Marshall, Wild's sledging partner in Shackleton's 1907–1909 try for the Pole. *Mills.*

Crean. County Kerry

"One morning Crean called me to say he had seen a seal only about 150 yards away, & I rushed out with the rifle.... Visibility was bad, at most fifty yards, but presently Crean pointed out the seal, partially hidden behind some ice hummocks.... I levelled the rifle...& was actually pressing the trigger when the seal rose upright & to our horror proved to be one of the scientists who, being of a modest nature, had chosen this spot instead of our usual retiring shelter." *Wild (Memoirs)*. *ML*.

"The Boss is a splendid gentleman and I done my duty towards him to the end." Crean, in a letter to Apsley Cherry-Garrard, 21 September 1917. *SPRI*. Quoted in *Alexander*.

Crean was born in County Kerry and returned there after the *Endurance* to open a pub: The South Pole Inn.

In February 1912, during Scott's attempt to reach the Pole, Crean, William Lashly, and Lt. "Teddy" Evans were the last party sent back to base camp by Scott, who went on with four others. Nearly one hundred miles from the Hut Point base, Evans collapsed with scurvy and was dragged on the sledge by Lashly and Crean. Finally, Crean hiked alone thirty miles over the ice to get help, carrying only three biscuits and two sticks of chocolate. It took him twenty hours.

South African Birds

A hadeda (pronounced *ha'-dee-dah*) is a South African ibis, the only ibis that is not silent; its call is a raucous "ha ha haa de daa."

Acknowledgments

IN ADDITION to permissions for published work credited on the copyright page, the author acknowledges the generosity of the following individuals and institutions.

Many of the men's journals, letters, and memoirs remain unpublished, and are held by libraries and research institutions. Permission to quote from the journals of Frank Worsley, Thomas Orde-Lees, and Harry McNeish and from Frank Wild's letter to Miss Anderson was given by the Alexander Turnbull Library of the National Library of New Zealand. The Scott Polar Research Institute granted permission to quote from interviews by James Fisher, Ernest Shackleton's papers, the journals of Lionel Greenstreet and Reginald James, Wild's journal of the 1907–1909 Antarctic expedition, a letter written by Tom Crean, Worsley's navigational log, and Orde-Lees' unpublished memoir ("Beset by Berg and Floe"). The Mitchell Library of the State Library of New South Wales gave permission for use of Frank Hurley's journal and Wild's unpublished memoir. The Royal Geographical Society of South Australia granted permission to quote from a letter written by Wild to Augusta James. Full bibliographic information and further details about the sources of quotations are in the endnotes.

The kindest permissions were those given by families of expedition members to quote from their relatives' papers. I am grateful to Mrs. Anne Fright (Frank Wild's niece), Mr. Sandy Macklin (Alexander Macklin's son), and Mrs. Toni Mooy (Frank Hurley's daughter) for their generosity in this regard. I would also like to thank Mr. Richard H. Greenstreet for sharing reminiscences about his uncle and other members of the expedition, and for helping to clarify the provenance of some of the expedition papers.

Tracking down these materials and their copyright holders required the aid of a number of archivists and librarians. My gratitude for their patient assistance goes to Valerie Sitters (Royal Geographical Society of South Australia), Dr. Robert Headland (Scott Polar Research Institute), Jennifer Broomhead, Kevin Leamon, and Paul Brunton of the Mitchell Library, Mr. Huw Thomas (Royal Geographical Society, London), and Robin Gyles and David Retter of the

Alexander Turnbull Library. I am also grateful to Leif Mills, Wild's biographer, for his assistance.

Every effort has been made to contact the copyright holders of the excerpted material used in this book. If there are any errors or omissions, please contact Van West & Company so that these can be corrected in any future editions. I have been unable to trace copyright holders for the papers of Reginald James, William Bakewell, and Thomas Orde-Lees. I will be grateful if their descendants, survivors, or estate executors get in touch with me in care of my publisher.

My heartfelt thanks go to my editor, Mary Jane Knecht, and my publisher, Jenny Van West, for helping to make this a better book than I could ever have made it by myself. David Caligiuri and Amy Smith Bell have my gratitude for their Herculean copyediting labors.

For making the author a better person than I could ever have made her by myself, I thank Gayle Pearl, Anne Pitkin, Rob Phillips, Jen Bandy-Phillips, Garrett Bandy, Julianne Seeman, Philip Chen, Jack O'Connell and family, Heidi Neff and family, and my colleagues and students.

Ultimate thanks for this book must go to those who lived this story, the men of the Imperial Trans-Antarctic Expedition.

About the Author

MELINDA MUELLER has published three previous collections of poetry: *Apocrypha* (Grey Spider Press, 1998), *Private Gallery* (Seal Press, 1976), and *Asleep in Another Country* (Jawbone Press, 1979), which received a Washington State Governor's Award. Her poems have been included in the *Pushcart Prize XX* and *Best American Poetry 1990* anthologies and in many literary journals. Born in Helena, Montana, she now lives in Seattle, where she teaches high school biology at Seattle Academy.

BOOK DESIGN AND COMPOSITION by Jennifer Van West. The text type is Baskerville with Mrs. Eaves titles. *Printed by McNaughton & Gunn.*